Teaching Hope and Resilience for Students Experiencing Trauma

Teaching Hope and Resilience for Students Experiencing Trauma

CREATING SAFE AND NURTURING
CLASSROOMS FOR LEARNING

Douglas Fisher
Nancy Frey
Rachelle S. Savitz

TEACHERS COLLEGE PRESS

TEACHERS COLLEGE | COLUMBIA UNIVERSITY
NEW YORK AND LONDON

Published by Teachers College Press, 1234 Amsterdam Avenue, New York, NY 10027

Portions of this book were drawn from previously published works, including:

Fisher, D. (2005). The literacy educator's role in suicide prevention. *Journal of Adolescent and Adult Literacy, 48*, 364–373.

Fisher, D. (2006). Responding to students who disclose the violence in their lives? *English Journal, 95*(6), 65–70.

Frey, N., & Fisher, D. (2008). The underappreciated role of humiliation in middle school. *Middle School Journal, 39*(5), 4–13

Cover design by Patricia Palao. Cover photo by Vichien Petchmai / Getty Images.

Library of Congress Cataloging-in-Publication Data

Names: Fisher, Douglas, 1965- author.
Title: Teaching hope and resilience for students experiencing trauma : creating safe and nurturing classrooms for learning / Douglas Fisher, Nancy Frey, Rachelle Savitz.
Description: New York : Teachers College Press, [2020] | Includes bibliographical references and index.
Identifiers: LCCN 2019030159 (print) | LCCN 2019030160 (ebook) | ISBN 9780807761984 (hardcover) | ISBN 9780807761472 (paperback) | ISBN 9780807777848 (ebook)
Subjects: LCSH: Mentally ill children—Education. | Teachers—Training of. | Psychic trauma in children. | Affective education. | School environment—Psychological aspects.
Classification: LCC LC4165 .F57 2019 (print) | LCC LC4165 (ebook) | DDC 371.94—dc23
LC record available at https://lccn.loc.gov/2019030159
LC ebook record available at https://lccn.loc.gov/2019030160

ISBN 978-0-8077-6147-2 (paper)
ISBN 978-0-8077-6198-4 (hardcover)
ISBN 978-0-8077-7784-8 (ebook)

Printed on acid-free paper
Manufactured in the United States of America

Contents

Introduction
Trauma, Teaching, and Learning

Caring and effective educators see the whole child. Each young person brings with them a host of experiences, a rich cultural history, and a unique combination of dispositions that inform their view of the world and themselves. As their teachers, we understand that we are not simply the dispensers of subject knowledge. Every interaction we have with them shapes students' perceptions of themselves and their place in the world.

Our influence on our students is awe-inspiring and humbling. In fact, the power we hold to impact the learning lives of our students can be paralyzing. Perhaps it is due to the notion that with great power comes great responsibility (you may attribute this to Voltaire or to Spider-Man creator Stan Lee, as is your preference). Our ability to influence the trajectory of a child's life is profound. And quite frankly, it is psychologically easier to retreat to a false belief that we have little power than it is to fully confront the responsibility we have to use our collective power for the betterment of young humans.

We have the power to create schools that are places of learning about oneself and the world for all students, and safe harbors for those whose lives are chaotic. We have the power to use our relationships with students to build their sense of agency so that they can take command of their destiny. We have the power to weave social and emotional learning (SEL) into every moment of the school day, not just on Thursday afternoons during the designated SEL lesson. We have the power to leverage the literacies of reading, writing, speaking, listening, and viewing as tools to help children and youth navigate their lives. We have the power to create safe communities that include everyone and preclude, to the greatest extent possible, any individual from becoming dangerously isolated. We have the power to build resilience in our students to help them withstand trauma. We have the power to use our schools as a launching pad for a call to action in their communities, and in the process as a means to heal themselves. In other words, we have the power to assist students in seeing the power that we see in them. But how might we activate that power? That is the purpose of this book.

PERSONAL TRAUMA AND ITS LASTING EFFECTS

Just before the turn of the current century, the results of a ground-breaking study were released, and as a result the conversation about traumatic experiences changed forever. Researchers at Kaiser Permanente partnered with medical investigators to examine the association between childhood abuse and adult health risks and disease (Felitti et al., 1998). More than 8,500 adults seeking health care services responded to questionnaires about childhood exposure to physical, sexual, and substance abuse in the household, as well as instances of mental illness and criminal behavior in the immediate family. The researchers statistically correlated these exposures to adult risk-taking to health and the prevalence of disease. Perhaps most important, the results of the study demonstrated that the number of childhood exposures correlated to an increased likelihood of negative health consequences in adulthood (e.g., substance abuse, depression, alcoholism, number of sexual intercourse partners). Subsequent studies identified a dose–response relationship between adverse childhood experiences (ACEs) of abuse, neglect, and violence, and adult social, health, and behavioral problems. In other words, there is a cumulative effect: An increase in the number of adverse experiences correlates to increased

Figure I.1. Adverse Childhood Experience (ACE) Questionnaire

Finding your ACE Score

While you were growing up, during your first 18 years of life:

1. Did a parent or other adult in the household often . . .

Swear at you, insult you, put you down, or humiliate you? or Act in a way that made you afraid that you might be physically hurt?

Yes / No   If yes enter 1 _____

2. Did a parent or other adult in the household often . . .

Push, grab, slap, or throw something at you? or Ever hit you so hard that you had marks or were injured?

Yes / No   If yes enter 1 _____

Figure I.1. Adverse Childhood Experience (ACE) Questionnaire (continued)

3. Did an adult or person at least 5 years older than you ever . . .

Touch or fondle you or have you touch their body in a sexual way? or Try to or actually have oral, anal, or vaginal sex with you?

Yes / No   If yes enter 1 _____

4. Did you often feel that . . .

No one in your family loved you or thought you were important or special? Or your family didn't look out for each other, feel close to each other, or support each other?

Yes / No   If yes enter 1 _____

5. Did you often feel that . . .

You didn't have enough to eat, had to wear dirty clothes, and had no one to protect you? or Your parents were too drunk or high to take care of you or take you to the doctor if you needed it?

Yes / No   If yes enter 1 _____

6. Were your parents ever separated or divorced?

Yes / No   If yes enter 1 _____

7. Was your mother or stepmother:

Often pushed, grabbed, slapped, or had something thrown at her? or Sometimes or often kicked, bitten, hit with a fist, or hit with something hard? or Ever repeatedly hit over at least a few minutes or threatened with a gun or knife?

Yes / No   If yes enter 1 _____

8. Did you live with anyone who was a problem drinker or alcoholic or who used street drugs?

Yes / No   If yes enter 1 _____

9. Was a household member depressed or mentally ill or did a household member attempt suicide?

Yes / No   If yes enter 1 _____

10. Did a household member go to prison?

Yes / No   If yes enter 1 _____

Now add up your "Yes" answers: _____   This is your ACE Score

Reprinted from *American Journal of Preventive Medicine*, 56(6). Vincent J. Felitti, Robert F. Anda, Dale Nordenberg, David F. Williamson, Alison M. Spitz, Valerie Edwards, Mary P. Koss, and James S. Marks. "Relationship of Childhood Abuse and Household Dysfunction to Many of the Leading Causes of Death in Adults: The Adverse Childhood Experiences (ACE) Study" (pp. 774-786). Copyright 2019 with permission from Elsevier.

risk of adult health problems. More recent studies have correlated ACEs to suicide, smoking, sleep disturbances, poor dental health, and suboptimal pregnancy outcomes (Centers for Disease Control and Prevention [CDC], n.d.). A simple 10-item questionnaire about experiences before the age of 18 is widely used to chronicle adverse childhood experiences (see Figure I.1).

We include this scoring tool for information about the cumulative effects of trauma on our students, not as a survey for teachers to administer to students. Answering such a questionnaire without support of counseling might in itself be traumatizing. In addition, students would need to be advised in advance that their reporting might require that the education professional, as a legally mandated reporter, would need to notify authorities.

TRAUMA AND ITS EFFECTS ON YOUNG PEOPLE

Trauma is described across three subtypes: acute, chronic, and complex traumas (Cook et al., 2005). Acute traumas are single events, such as the death of a parent. Chronic traumas occur repeatedly for a longer period of time, such as witnessing multiple incidences of a mother's physical abuse. Complex traumas emanate from chronic traumas and are interpersonal in nature. These are long-lasting, involve multiple traumatic events, and are perpetrated by immediate family members. As one example, the alcoholism of a caregiver, domestic violence in the household, sexual abuse victimization of the child, and the loss of a parent together weave a complex tapestry of mistrust and instability.

The sheer volume of traumatic events experienced by our students is staggering. In addition to the experiences outlined in the ACEs, searing events of homelessness, poverty, and discrimination contribute to a child's sense of victimization. The results of one national survey reported that 64.5% of children ages 2–17 experienced at least one victimization event *in a single year* (Finkelhor, Ormrod, & Turner, 2007). In other words, childhood experiences of trauma, whether acute, chronic, or complex, should be understood as being the norm rather than the exception.

The body's response to trauma is the well-known decision pathway of flight/fight/freeze. The release of stress hormones associated with these responses bathes the brain in chemicals that interfere with learning. Diminished learning is witnessed academically in the following ways:

- Thwarted development of language and communication skills
- Less attention to directions about task completion
- Inability to mentally organize new information
- Lower understanding of cause-and-effect relationships (Cole, Eisner, Gregory, & Ristuccia, 2013)

These are the fundamental tools of learning, and a teacher's reduced access to these cognitive channels results in lower student achievement and an increased potential for school failure and mental illness (McLeod, Uemura, & Rohrman, 2012).

BUT PAST IS NOT PROLOGUE

While the news on the prevalence and effects of trauma is sobering, it is crucial to remember that experience is not destiny. The relationship between ACEs and negative health, social, and learning behaviors should not be misunderstood as a *fait accompli*. In fact, the last thing that children who have experienced trauma need is pity and low expectations about their future. What they do need is empathy and a path forward. One student at the high school where two of us work was a reminder to us about this truth. The details of her traumatic experiences are not the point; suffice it to say that her childhood has been riddled with barriers that take our breath away. But this resilient and empowered young woman reminded us, "I am not my trauma. It doesn't define me. *I* define me."

In fact, resilience can be fostered through school experiences. Nearly 1,800 children who had experienced maltreatment before the age of 3 were followed through the age of 10. Protective factors (variables that reduce negative effects) that resulted in improved language and academic outcomes included:

- Access to preschool education
- Warmth and responsiveness of teachers and caregivers
- Prosocial skills, such as cooperation with peers, showing empathy, and being assertive
- Connectedness to the community (Holmes, Yoon, Berg, Cage, & Perzynski, 2018)

Resilience, which is the ability to successfully adapt "despite challenging or threatening circumstances" (Masten, Best, & Garmezy, 1990, p. 425), is not innate. Rather, it is fostered through conditions present in the environment. School is a primary environment for students and occupies a significant portion of time in their lives. School conditions that foster resilience among children include:

- Caring relationships with peers and adults
- Clear and high academic expectations
- Culturally sustaining pedagogy that honors cultural experiences, provides structure and boundaries, and uses group processes (Benard, 2004)

The very good news is that these are factors within our direct control. A hope-filled school, and the classrooms within it, can serve to counterbalance the circumstances that harm children and diminish their sense of self. As educators, we can use instructional practices and materials that foster the kind of resilience that our students need. We are able to socially engineer our classrooms to provide structure and choice so that students feel safe enough to make decisions. We can develop the social and emotional capacities of all children so that they can weather the storms of daily life. And importantly, having supported these strengths, we can teach our students how their voices can be used to engage in civic action and service.

THE PURPOSE OF THIS BOOK

Our classrooms and schools can be a safe haven for students. They can be spaces filled with warmth and an academic press for excellence. School should be a place where we utilize humane and growth-producing methods to help all children realize their promise. But this is possible only if we do so with intentionality. The chapters that follow serve as a road map for creating uniformly excellent classrooms and schools.

Chapter 1 focuses on the fundamental importance of teacher–student relationships. These are foundational to any learning that follows, as personal regard and responsiveness signal to children that they matter.

Chapter 2 addresses the ways in which *social and emotional learning* can be woven into the school day. It has been noted that whether we intend to or not, we teach our students SEL in every interaction. This chapter begins with a discussion of identity and agency, and extends to prosocial skills necessary for peer relationships, bullying prevention, and suicide prevention approaches.

In *Chapter 3* we turn our attention to the ways in which *literacies can be levers to maximize learning*, especially for traumatized youth. Through the use of powerful and purposeful reading of informational and narrative texts, discussion of sensitive and broad student concerns about topics like violence and deportation, writing as catharsis, and inquiry, we explore ways to simultaneously teach and heal.

Chapter 4 is dedicated to teaching through *learner empowerment*. One of the most debilitating side effects of trauma is loss of agency. This chapter engages with notions of debate, civics, and service learning as pathways for taking back control.

Chapter 5 discusses the vital nature of the *school community as an agent of change*. Families and communities possess the collective power to restore and inspire. Trauma-sensitive schools are a vital conduit for organizing efforts, supporting families experiencing trauma, and mobilizing community resources.

We are filled with hope, and we want educators to share our sense of possibility as we seek to better serve children who have experienced, or continue to experience, trauma in their lives. It is never easy. But who among us decided to enter this profession because we thought it would be easy? Your everyday courage makes a difference in the lives of young people. You give us hope.

CHAPTER 1

The Protective Power of Relationships

Josué is a 7th-grader who struggles in and out of school. A chaotic childhood littered with substance abuse and criminal activity in the family has resulted in the boy's constant changes in residence. He has lived with different caregivers, meaning that he often has had to change schools. Josué transferred to his current middle school in the month of February. He has a learning disability, and at the transfer IEP meeting held a day earlier, his aunt disclosed that while Josué has prescription eyeglasses, he refuses to wear them. When asked why, he mumbled a nonanswer, then looked away and sighed deeply.

Middle school, most adults will admit, is rarely easy. Early adolescence is a time of upheaval emotionally, psychologically, and physically for even the most secure children. For a boy like Josué, navigating middle school is exponentially more difficult. He has racked up a significant number of adverse childhood experiences, which are further compounded by an unstable home life and attendance at six different schools in the past 4 years. It is difficult to get much traction on addressing his learning disability given the frequent changes in schooling. Josué's survival mechanism is finely tuned: Keep your head down, don't draw attention to yourself, and don't bother to form relationships with other people. They just leave anyway.

But this middle school is different. The staff knows that students who enroll after the school year has begun are vulnerable to social isolation. These children are identified immediately to all the adults in the school, so that they can begin to form relationships. "It makes a difference when someone calls you by your name," remarked school custodian Elena Diaz, one of the school's first points of contact for any new child.

Despite his resistance, Josué can't help but be drawn to Charles Jackson, a magnetic member of the school's student support team.

Mr. Jackson is primarily involved in the school's restorative practices, an alternative to traditional discipline procedures (Smith, Fisher, & Frey, 2015). But he makes it his business to build relationships with as many students as possible. "It makes restoration much easier, if a problem arises, when there's already a connection there," he said. Mr. Jackson is a young, athletic man, and he towers over Josué. The morning after the IEP meeting, Mr. Jackson was waiting for the boy. "Hey, how are you, Josué?" he said in a booming voice, followed by an elaborate handshake routine that the student was still mastering. "Do you notice anything different about me today?" asked Mr. Jackson, smiling and pointing to his own eyeglasses. "I heard you weren't sure if cool guys wore glasses, so I'm going to not wear my contacts for a while. I'll wear my glasses, and you wear yours. Deal?" Josué smiled and nodded. "Us cool guys gotta stick together. Am I right?" waved Mr. Jackson. As the boy turned to walk to his first class, he paused, opened his backpack, and retrieved his own glasses. "That's what I'm talkin' about!" bellowed Mr. Jackson.

It is a small interaction, to be sure, and we would never suggest that this one event will build Josué's confidence in himself and his world. But put this in the context of many interactions with lots of adults every day. Ms. Diaz, for instance, will stop by the lunch table and greet Josué, just to ask him how his day is going. Margaret Holden, the vice principal, will share a flyer with him about the after-school gaming club and invite him to check it out. Lisa Sanchez, the parent relations coordinator at the school, will place a call to Josué's aunt to share positive news about the boy's math placement exam. In a hope-filled school like the one Josué now attends, developing, maintaining, and repairing relationships are viewed as being the central mission of every adult. Without foundational relationships with adults and peers, learning is thwarted. "If they can't trust, they can't learn," said Mr. Jackson. "What we do as a staff is invest in building trusting relationships, so they can access learning."

RELATIONSHIPS AND TRAUMATIZED YOUTH

Traumatized youth are notably distrustful of relationships with others. The neural pathways that form in the brain during the first few years of life set the stage for how relationships are perceived. Children who experience abuse and neglect are especially vulnerable to forming faulty neural pathways that distort their perceptions of relationships. For traumatized children, relationships are a threat. They rapidly toggle between past experience and predictions about what will occur next, in an attempt to make a decision about whether to trust or not. This "management of fear and anxiety," writes neuropsychology researcher Louis Cozolino (2014), "remains the core component of . . . attachment relationships" (p. 20).

The result of living in a steady state of fear and anxiety is hypervigilance. Children and youth who are hypervigilant may exhibit behaviors such as fidgeting, scanning the horizon, acting aggressively, or withdrawing from human contact and interaction. But it is what's happening inside that presents the true barrier to learning. The stress chemicals that are released block access to the cerebral cortex, which is the thinking part of the brain—the place where problem solving and strategic decision making occur (Leitch, 2017).

Yet it is the restorative nature of relationships that lies at the heart of trauma-informed care. Forming positive relationships is an essential pathway that leads a troubled child toward a more resilient future self. And it is up to adults to lead the way so that children can develop a set of healthy emotional habits. The very good news is that as children gain experiences with positive relationships, new neural pathways replace the older ones. The neuroplasticity of the brain, which is to say, the ability of the brain to rewire itself, is a possibility for all people. While the capability of the brain to reorganize itself persists across a lifetime, the brain is especially adept at doing so in childhood and adolescence.

TEACHER–STUDENT RELATIONSHIPS

The influence of teacher–student relationships on learning is powerful, with an effect size of 0.52 (Hattie, 2018). Effect size is a statistical tool that reports the magnitude of one variable's effect on another variable. A year's worth of academic progress is calculated at 0.40; influences reported above this "hinge point" are likely to speed learning. Hattie's calculation of effect size of teacher–student relationships on student learning is drawn from dozens of meta-analyses on the subject.

The characteristics of positive teacher–student relationships speak to the context of schooling. These should not be confused with friendships, which are relationships with peers. Rather, adults at school, whether they are in credentialed or certificated positions, promote strong positive relationships with students through the following channels:

Relatedness through demonstration of interest in a student's life

Providing reliable structures and boundaries by creating fair and consistent expectations and rules that govern interactions

Autonomous conditions that allow for student choice and opportunities to make decisions that matter

Optimism about students, which is infused in communication with children about beliefs in them as learners and people

Emotional support, especially in acknowledging feelings and assisting children in processing emotions

Teacher emotional support, autonomy, and relatedness are associated with higher degrees of motivation and engagement in adolescents, which themselves are two essential drivers of learning (Ruzek et al., 2016). In their study of nearly 1,000 students ages 11–17, the researchers found that student reports of emotionally supportive classrooms, defined as those characterized by "teachers' demonstration of genuine concern for and care about their students, respect for their students, desire to understand students' feelings and points of views, and dependability," were linked to positive perceptions about students' mastery motivation and behavioral engagement (p. 95). Students in these classrooms reported that they possessed personal goals for learning and strived to listen carefully, participate in discussions, and do well academically. The teachers who exhibited high degrees of emotional support used a cluster of behaviors that the researchers termed "regard for adolescent perspectives," namely:

- Encouraging student ideas and opinions
- Connecting content to students' lives
- Maintaining a relaxed structure for movement about the classroom
- Using peer-sharing and group-work

These teaching behaviors, intentionally enacted by adults, can promote strong positive relationships because they are all within our locus of control.

DIFFERENTIAL TREATMENT OF STUDENTS

But the troubling fact is that while all of us readily can point to evidence of positive relationships with individual students, those relationships are not evenly distributed. We are humans before we are educators, and we easily connect with those people for whom we have an affinity. But students who have experienced trauma may exhibit exactly the kinds of behaviors that *don't* draw us to them. They avoid our gaze and rarely speak to us unless it is about a task or direction. Or they act out in ways that cause us to avoid contact with them. Keep in mind that these are the markers of a hypervigilant child who doesn't trust the world. Our subsequent avoidance of them simply validates what they already may believe about themselves and others: that they are not worthy, and emotional investment in others is not worth it, either.

Although we don't like to admit it, the evidence is that students who are identified as being low-achieving are treated differently by their teachers. Good (1987) found differential teacher behaviors between low- and high-achieving students. Students identified as low-achieving:

- Were provided less wait time to answer questions.
- Received less eye contact from the teacher.
- Received more criticism for failure.
- Received less praise and feedback from the teacher.
- Were seated further away from the teacher.
- Had fewer interactions of any kind with the teacher.

The quality of teacher interactions, in turn, negatively impacts the child. Limited and negative interactions with teachers increase the likelihood that students will exhibit problematic behaviors. Also, they adopt negative attitudes about themselves and believe that their teachers have lower expectations for them (Montague & Rinaldi, 2001).

A two-pronged study of the long-term effects of negative teacher interactions is illustrative. Researchers studied teacher interactions with kindergarten and 1st-grade students, using an instrument designed to quantify the differential behaviors described by Good (1987). Students were identified as being either at risk or not at risk for developing emotional and behavioral disorders. Children also were interviewed about their perceptions of themselves and the teacher. Examination of those same students in 3rd and 4th grades found that negative teacher interactions in the primary grades accurately predicted subsequent negative treatment by their teachers in the intermediate grades and deepened the negative beliefs the at-risk children had about themselves and their teachers (Montague & Rinaldi, 2001).

Negative teacher interactions have a further chilling effect on relationships with classmates. Children who experience negative teacher interactions are rejected by peers more readily (Birch & Ladd, 1997). A study of more than 1,400 5th-grade students found that peers were able to accurately perceive whether their teachers liked another student (or not). These student perceptions were discerned through observation of verbal and nonverbal teacher behaviors. Most troubling of all is that peers reliably reported that they also disliked the targeted child and that this perception persisted 6 months later (Hendrickx, Mainhard, Oudman, Boor-Klip, & Brekelmans, 2017). This phenomenon, called social referencing, describes the influence a teacher has on peer perceptions. Interestingly, the reverse is not the case. Positive teacher behaviors did not influence peer approval. But when it comes to negative perceptions, children watch the teacher closely to determine who should not be liked. In other words, teachers are a compass for peer rejection. Not being liked by peers has a strong negative influence on students. Hattie (2018) reports a negative influence of -0.19 for not being liked in school, equivalent to about half a year's worth of learning lost in a school year.

THE DAMAGING EFFECTS OF HUMILIATION AND SARCASM

In his book *The World Is Flat*, Friedman (2005) argued that we have underappreciated the role that humiliation plays in terrorism. He notes that the reaction humans have when they are humiliated is significant and often severe. If it is true that humiliation plays a role in terrorism, what role might this underappreciated emotion play in school? If terrorists act, in part, based on humiliation, how do students act when they experience this emotion? From resentfulness to rage, humiliation can spark a range of destructive acts to self or others.

To answer these questions, we interviewed 10 middle school teachers and 10 students (Frey & Fisher, 2008). We asked teachers about times either they (or their students) were humiliated and asked students about times they (or their peers) were humiliated, and what happened. In each case, they were surprised to be asked about this emotion. They all said things like, "It just happens; you gotta deal with it." The responses from the teachers and students about the ways that students are humiliated were illuminating.

Student Voices About Humiliation and Sarcasm

Students interviewed had strong feelings about the use of humiliation by teachers. Nine of the 10 student participants could recount times when a teacher had used sarcasm or humiliation to embarrass a student in front of the class. In some cases it was directed at them, while in others they had witnessed it in their classes:

> We had this one teacher in 7th grade; man, she was rough. She had a nickname for every kid in the class. Like, she called this one girl "Funeral," because she said she always looked like she was coming from one.

This story, told by Al, is admittedly an extreme example and not typical of the incidences that were shared by students. However, three students told of times when teachers had "busted someone" in front of the entire class for failing a quiz or test, using insulting language. "I don't know why they do it," said Gail, a 6th-grader. "It's not like it makes a difference. Who wants to work harder for someone who embarrasses you that way?"

Veronica, an 8th-grade student, said:

> Ms. _____ likes to catch you doing something wrong. Like, we were reading our social studies book out loud and I missed my turn. She goes, "Wake up, Veronica! We're all waiting," in this really stupid way she has [imitates a sarcastic tone]. Everyone laughed as though it never happened to them. I don't let her catch me.

Veronica then used profanity to describe her teacher, evidence of the anger she felt toward this adult and perhaps school in general.

Other students admitted that the use of humiliation might have a positive effect, at least in the short term:

My [7th-grade] math teacher reads everyone's quiz grades to the whole class. I failed one, and he said, "Spending too much time looking at girls?" It made me kinda mad . . . but I made sure I didn't fail another math quiz. (Juan, 8th grade)

When students were asked what they thought these teachers hoped to gain with the use of humiliation, their insights were surprising. "They want to be cool, like it's funny," remarked 6th-grade student Marcus. Seventh-grader Harlan responded similarly. "They don't treat you like little kids. My dad talks the same way. Making fun of kids in the class is just what they do."

Teacher Voices About Humiliation and Sarcasm

The use of sarcasm and humiliation by teachers has been less well documented in the literature, although it certainly has been long understood in the teaching profession, as evidenced by Briggs's (1928) article on the prevalence of the use of sarcasm by young secondary teachers. Martin's (1987) study of secondary students' perspectives on this phenomenon was derived from surveys of more than 20,000 Canadian students.

In that study, students reported that the use of sarcasm resulted in dislike for the teacher and even anger toward the teacher. Some students also described "anticipatory embarrassment," the dread associated with the belief that the teacher would humiliate them again. In addition, this created learning problems, including decreased motivation to study and complete homework, increased cutting of classes, and thoughts of dropping out. Turner and associates (2002) studied the classroom learning environments of 65 6th-grade mathematics classrooms to identify factors that promoted or reduced help-seeking behaviors. They found that the teacher's classroom discourse, including use of sarcasm, influenced the likelihood that students would seek academic help when needed. Classrooms featuring more negative teacher talk, including sarcasm, were associated with high levels of avoidance in asking for assistance.

Six of the 10 teachers in our study named colleagues who regularly used sarcasm and humiliation with students. Ms. Robertson, a 7th-grade language arts teacher, described a colleague as "us[ing] words like a knife. He just cuts kids down to size." Mr. Lee, a math teacher, described an experience when he was a student teacher:

[The master teacher] was just vicious with students. Everything was a big joke, but kind of mean-spirited, you know? He'd single out kids because of a quirk, like they talked funny, or they had a big nose, or they wore clothes that were kind of different. Kids would laugh, but I saw the cringes, too.

Five of the participating teachers discussed the fine line between humor and sarcasm. Ms. Andersen offered:

You have to take into account that they're really very fragile, in spite of all their bluster. We all remember what it was like. Worried all the time about sticking out. They're already sensitive to the need for conformity. As teachers, we have to make sure that we don't make them feel different.

Ms. Hartford noted, "It's great to keep it light and fun, but not at someone else's expense." Sarcasm typically is used for three purposes: to soften a criticism, especially through feigned politeness; to mitigate verbal aggressiveness; or to create humor (Dews & Winner, 1995). However, the use of sarcasm in social discourse assumes an equal relationship between parties. This is never the case in the classroom, where the teacher holds the power in the relationship. Therefore, the student cannot respond with a sarcastic reply without consequences. The use of sarcasm with middle school students is ineffective as well, as evidenced by a study of 13-year-olds by Harvard Project Zero. The researchers found that 71% of the students studied misinterpreted sarcasm as deception, believing that the teacher was tricking them and not clearly stating expectations. In other words, the majority had not yet reached a linguistically sophisticated developmental level that would allow them to accurately discern the speaker's purpose, even when it was accompanied by a gestural cue (Demorest, Meyer, Phelps, Gardner, & Winner, 1984).

Humiliation and Attendance Problems

Another outcome of humiliation, discussed by both students and teachers in the study, was poor school attendance. Mr. Harper, the music teacher, put it eloquently: "They vote with their feet"—meaning that students tell us, by their physical presence in school, whether or not it is a comfortable place to be. Again, most educators acknowledge that there are patterns of problematic attendance, such as typically is seen in urban schools. More important, for our purpose here, is the difference in attendance patterns within a school. It is clear from an analysis of attendance patterns—both tardiness and absence—that students are communicating which teachers they do and do not feel comfortable with. While there are many reasons for students feeling comfortable with teachers, one reason is the climate that is created in class. Veronica reported, "Lots of us cut class with Mr. _____ because he makes you feel bad when you try to answer."

Humiliation and Dropping Out

While calculating an accurate dropout rate has been exceedingly difficult to do, it is important to note that until recently there has been no mechanism for capturing middle school dropouts in many states. It seems that when the data systems were created, people assumed that middle school students either would not or could not drop out of school.

Unfortunately, that is not the reality; middle school students are dropping out. In-grade retention (an indicator of either poor academic performance or poor attendance) is the single strongest school-related predictor of dropping out in middle school (Rumberger, 1995). As Ms. Indria reported, "There are students who just leave us. They don't find school fulfilling and are ashamed of their performance, and they stop coming. No one really knows where they go." Turner and associates' (2002) study on the relationship between classroom climate and help-seeking offers further evidence of the role of humiliation. There is also evidence that the overall school climate—the degree to which students feel safe to learn and are not threatened by peers or teachers—is directly related to the dropout problem (Kotok, Ikoma, & Bodovski, 2016). As Al indicated, "If I had to deal with the crap that Jeremy does, I'd just quit. I wouldn't come to this place."

School institutional structures related to humiliation are a factor as well. According to Goldschmidt and Wang (1999), "Two school policy and practice variables affect the middle school dropout rate significantly: the percentage of students held back one grade, and the percentage of students misbehaving" (p. 728). Here we see the snowballing effects of humiliation. Students retained in grade, attending remedial classes, surrounded by misbehavior (including bullying), with lower rates of attendance and less inclination to seek help from sarcastic teachers, appear to be at great risk for dropping out, and humiliation plays a role in each of those factors.

It is time to notice our own behaviors and to have hard conversations with our colleagues about appropriate interactions with students—interactions that clearly demonstrate care, honesty, and high expectations. In doing so, we might just see increases in student achievement as well as youth who are more engaged in their educational experience.

INTERRUPT THE PATTERN

Whether the negative impact of differential treatment, humiliation, and sarcasm is causational or correlational seems beside the point. The real question is, "How might we interrupt these patterns?" The Teacher Expectations and Student Achievement (TESA) framework, designed by the Los Angeles County Office of Education (LACOE), has had nearly 40 years of success in changing how teachers interact with students who are low-achieving, are negatively perceived, and exhibit problematic behaviors. The framework is informed by three principles that change interaction behaviors:

> **Response opportunities** to increase academic interactions
> **Feedback** to provide learners with validation and positive reinforcement
> **Personal regard** to build positive teacher–student relationships (LACOE, 2008)

The premise is simple, but the execution is not. The designers of the program invite teachers to identify three students with whom they have problematic relationships, and then systematically and intentionally change the nature of the interactions.

Principle 1: Increase Response Opportunities

Students are not called on in equal measure, nor are they always afforded the time, assistance, and cognitive challenge needed to move learning forward. Therefore, this first principle speaks to the questioning habits of teachers. There are five specific behaviors in the TESA framework that increase response opportunities. The first is *equitable distribution*, meaning that teachers should pay attention to ensuring that there is a balance across gender, ability, and physical location in the classroom. (The evidence is that students seated in the "T-zone," which comprises the front row and the center column of the classroom, get more chances to respond.) The second and third are *individual help* and *latency*, which refer to the scaffolds offered, as well as the wait time received, for students to fully formulate a response. The fourth is *delving*, which consists of asking the student a follow-up question to prompt further responses. The last teacher behavior is *higher-order questioning*, which means asking queries that encourage students to utilize critical thinking skills, rather than simply recall and reproduce information. The overall effect of changes in questioning behaviors is that the length and quality of interactions are increased.

Principle 2: Feedback

The five overt behaviors aligned with this principle are designed to shape how teachers respond to targeted students. The first is *affirming or correcting* student responses, which is the first step in providing feedback. The second and third are *praising* and *giving reasons for praise*. These are not hollow platitudes ("Good job!"), but rather positive statements that provide students with information they can utilize. Telling students, "I can see you really gave that a lot of thought," lets them know that you appreciate the depth of their comment. A fourth element is *listening*, which sometimes is referred to as wait time and refers to the pauses that come after a student responds. Listening also requires fully receiving the message delivered by the student, using your full attention. The fifth behavior is *acceptance of student feelings*. As noted in the Ruzek et al. (2016) study, adolescents in particular appreciate when teachers accept their perspectives and feelings. Students draw on acceptance of feelings as a source of motivation and engagement.

Principle 3: Personal Regard

This last constellation of teacher behaviors speaks to the ways in which we connect with others using pragmatic elements of communication. The first technique is *proximity*, which is the distance between the teacher and student. Culture, gender, personality, and prior experience influence personal preferences about proximity, and this can be especially true for children who have had traumatic experiences. Obviously, too close is a problem, as people often will react negatively if their personal space is violated. However, too much distance is actually a more frequent problem in classrooms, as negatively perceived students often are seated further away from the teacher and in a portion of the room that is infrequently inhabited by the teacher. A related nonverbal means of communication is *touching*. As with proximity, this should be approached carefully when working with a child with adverse childhood experiences. Having said that, touch is an important way in which we bond with other humans. Appropriate touch communicates affection and is viewed as an essential condition for growth and development.

Personal regard is further communicated verbally using *courtesy* and expressing *compliments and interest* in students. It is amazing how much mileage you can get out of building a relationship with a student in this way. We have advised using the 2 x 10 method to build communication (Wlodkowski, 1983). For 2 minutes a day, for 10 days in a row (2 weeks of school), strike up a conversation with the targeted student about anything except school. Ask them for a good music recommendation, or whether they follow a local sports team, or how they got to school this morning, really anything that breaks the ice and gets them talking, if only for a short time. In the process, you will find out something about the student that you can build upon. The final teacher behavior is *desisting*, which is the manner in which the teacher ends a problematic behavior in a calm and courteous way, with an eye toward returning the student to a productive state as quickly as possible. Conflicts between teachers and students predictably arise, and there should be a plan for how to respond constructively. This can be challenging, but it is infinitely easier when a positive relationship between the teacher and student already exists.

MEASURING TEACHER–STUDENT RELATIONSHIPS
THROUGH WARMTH AND CONFLICT

Teacher warmth and conflict have a direct influence on the academic achievement of students. That is, teacher warmth is a predictor of higher academic accomplishment; teacher conflict is a predictor of lower achievement (Jerome, Hamre, & Pianta, 2008). Perhaps even more important, the amount of closeness or conflict with a child predicts a teacher's rating of the student's academic achievement. In other words, the affection and closeness experienced between a teacher and a student influences the teacher's perception of the child's achievement and materially impacts the student's academic gains.

Students who have experienced adverse childhood experiences, as well as other related life stressors, including racism, immigration status, and family unemployment, are in particular need of emotionally supportive and warm teachers. Yet at-risk children are less often the recipients of teacher warmth. Split, Hughes, Wu, and Kwok (2012) followed 657 students from grades 1 through 6 who had been identified as being at risk. The researchers were interested in examining the influence of relational adversity (conflict) with their teachers and its possible effects on academic achievement. They reported that "African American children, children with early behavior problems, and children with low IQ were more likely to experience low warmth throughout elementary school" (p. 1190).

But these dynamics are directly within our control, should we choose to enact them. We can change the relationships we have with students, especially those who are already vulnerable. Pianta (1992) has developed and normed a short-form tool of 15 questions for teachers to use to interrogate their relationships (see Figure 1.1). The Student–Teacher Relationship Scale (STRS) asks teachers to consider their interactions with and reactions to individual students. Gauging one's own emotional responses can provide insight into which relationships need to be strengthened. "Dealing with this child drains my energy" (item 11), for instance, requires teachers to take a measure of their own emotional response. "When this child is in a bad mood, I know we're in for a long and difficult day" (item 12) asks teachers to consider how they make predictions about future behavior. The scale reports on two measures—closeness and conflict—and includes information about normative data and a scoring guide. These tools can be accessed at curry.virginia.edu/faculty-research/centers-labs-projects/castl/measures-developed-robert-c-pianta-phd.

The results of this scale can assist you in identifying students who might benefit from the TESA strategies described in the previous section. In acting intentionally to build, maintain, and repair relationships with vulnerable children, you will take an important first step in maximizing learning and promoting an emotionally safe school in an otherwise traumatized environment.

Figure 1.1. Student–Teacher Relationship Scale: Short Form

Child: _____

Teacher: _____ Grade:_____

Please reflect on the degree to which each of the following statements currently applies to your relationship with this child. Using the scale below, circle the appropriate number for each item.

Definitely does not apply	Not really	Neutral, not sure	Applies somewhat	Definitely applies
1	2	3	4	5

1.	I share an affectionate, warm relationship with this child.	1	2	3	4	5
2.	This child and I always seem to be struggling with each other.	1	2	3	4	5
3.	If upset, this child will seek comfort from me.	1	2	3	4	5
4.	This child is uncomfortable with physical affection or touch from me.	1	2	3	4	5
5.	This child values his/her relationship with me.	1	2	3	4	5
6.	When I praise this child, he/she beams with pride.	1	2	3	4	5
7.	This child spontaneously shares information about himself/herself.	1	2	3	4	5
8.	This child easily becomes angry with me.	1	2	3	4	5
9.	It is easy to be in tune with what this child is feeling.	1	2	3	4	5
10.	This child remains angry or is resistant after being disciplined.	1	2	3	4	5
11.	Dealing with this child drains my energy.	1	2	3	4	5
12.	When this child is in a bad mood, I know we're in for a long and difficult day.	1	2	3	4	5
13.	This child's feelings toward me can be unpredictable or can change suddenly.	1	2	3	4	5
14.	This child is sneaky or manipulative with me.	1	2	3	4	5
15.	This child openly shares his/her feelings and experiences with me.	1	2	3	4	5

THE WARM DEMANDER

We do vulnerable children no favors when we lower expectations for their learning. We are often the lens for helping them see the greatness within, even when they might not yet see it in themselves. A warm demander (Kleinfeld, 1975) is a teacher who couples strong relationships with high expectations. Teachers who are warm demanders utilize the nonverbal communication channels of touch, facial expressions, and proximity, and pair these techniques with personal regard behaviors such as showing interest and acknowledging feelings to build rapport. A warm demander is skilled at linking these to high academic expectations and goals (Ware, 2006). There is an academic press to strive, and students are held accountable for their actions and performance. These teachers are firm and direct in the way they speak to students, but are not sarcastic, threatening, or easy to anger. Their interactions with students are never demeaning or humiliating, as they seek to preserve the dignity of every child, especially when that child is not at their best.

We opened this chapter with a description of Mr. Jackson's relationship-building tactics with Josué. Mr. Jackson is a warm demander, as evidenced in another interaction he had with the same student the following week. As a member of the student support team at the middle school, Mr. Jackson is in classrooms regularly. He was in the boy's English class, where students were engaged in a timed writing prompt about a short story they had read, "Eleven" by Sandra Cisneros (1991). However, Josué was not writing. In fact, he seemed to be fiddling with his laptop and pestering peers—just all-around foolishness, but driven by the hypervigilance he has adopted as a coping mechanism. Mr. Jackson knelt down next to Josué's desk, looked the child in the eye, and in a low and firm voice said:

> You're not being the student I know you can be. Ms. West [the teacher] gave you directions. Are they confusing to you? If so, I can help. But now's the time to take a deep breath, settle yourself, and get to work. You've got 17 minutes left to show what you know.

Mr. Jackson held his gaze for a few more seconds, until Josué said, "I'm ready." After class, he apologized to Ms. West and to Mr. Jackson, who readily accepted the apology and praised him for pulling himself together. Ms. West, another warm demander, said, "You seemed to like this story, Josué. I'm looking forward to reading your thoughts. Then you and I can develop some goals about what you want to accomplish in this class, and what I want for you."

The notion of the teacher as warm demander initially resonated with schools in underserved communities. However, it is essential to note that children who have had adverse childhood experiences are not protected by race, socioeconomic status, urbanity, or any other number of ways that we commonly categorize communities. In fact, schools that *don't* actively seek to identify and serve students experiencing hardships leave these children particularly vulnerable to exploitation, abuse, and harm. These children hide in plain sight. Students understand that warm demanders telegraph to them that they are "important enough to be pushed, disciplined, helped, taught, and respected" (Wilson & Corbett, 2001, p. 88). Nothing is more soul-crushing than the realization that you just *don't matter* to anyone. Our warm demands tell students that we see them and they matter to us. Schools can and should be warm demanders, filled with adults who build relationships, hold high expectations, provide emotional support, and build the resilience of all students, especially those who have experienced trauma.

BUILD THE RESILIENCE OF STUDENTS
THROUGH STRONGER RELATIONSHIPS

Positive teacher–student relationships serve as an environmental protective factor against stress and risky behaviors, which are negative adaptations that stem from adverse experiences (O'Dougherty Wright, Masten, & Narayan, 2013). There is an inverse correlation between positive teacher–student relationships and risk behaviors for at-risk youth—the stronger the relationship, the less likely students are to engage in risky behavior (Sanders, Munford, & Liebenberg, 2016). Environmental factors are the structures and procedures we can establish to build students' internal protective factors (a concept we will discuss in more detail in the next chapter). Resilience rests on the relationships children have at home and at school. Hope-filled schools invest in structures that promote strong relationships. The following are practices that bolster positive relationships in hope-filled schools:

1. Ensure that every adult in the school receives annual training, ongoing coaching, and regular guidance to build and maintain relationships. Too often relationship-building professional learning is confined to the start of the school year and offered only to classroom teachers. But every adult has the potential to provide strong relational supports.

2. Develop and support mentorship programs at the school that pair caring educators with students. At the school where two of us work, every adult in the building has a dozen or so students assigned to them as mentees. At a hope-filled school, student mentorship is a part of every job description, including administrative, clerical, certificated, and credentialed positions.

3. Directly confront the use of humiliation and sarcasm by adults. The effects are damaging and undermine positive efforts. Administrators have a special duty to ensure that the school environment is a welcoming, humane, and growth-producing space for everyone. There is simply no room in a hope-filled school for adults to shame children.

4. Establish mechanisms for identifying troubled relationships between adults and students, and provide systems of support for both to repair these relationships. Restorative practices emphasize a key concept: *It's not rules that get violated; it's relationships that are violated when harm is done.* Adults and students need ongoing support, coaching, and guidance to mend and maintain relationships.

5. Examine and promote practices that foster warm demanders and a schoolwide sense of academic press. These practices include supporting teachers to develop classroom management skills that do not rely on punitive measures.

6. Work with families and caregivers to develop culturally sustaining practices for home and school that build strong relationships. While we will address this more thoroughly in Chapter 5, we don't want to wait until then to mention drawing on community assets. Hope-filled schools recognize that families and the larger community are the not-so-secret tools for building strong children.

Reflective Questions for You

At the end of each chapter, we will pose a few questions that invite you to reflect on your current practices and to set goals for continuous improvement. After all, hope-filled schools are created by adults who are themselves resilient and strive to be better each year.

- How am I communicating my expectations to my students?
- Are my expectations different for my "high," "average," and "low" achievers?
- In what ways does the ethnic, racial, or cultural background of my students affect my expectations for them? How do I know?
- During class, do I call on students of all abilities equally?
- Am I making an attempt to get to know each of my students on a personal level?

CHAPTER 2

Social and Emotional Learning Is Woven into the Curriculum

Maheera is a proud and self-possessed young woman at the school where two of us work. She joined us as a 7th-grade student and is now in her senior year. To say that this person lights up any room she is in would be an understatement. A quick smile, gentle humor, and a keen mind make her a favorite among peers and adults. She comes from a loving and supportive home, where the traditional Islamic values of faith, service, and community are reflected in her daily life. She is a thoroughly American teenager who wears a hajib, loves reality television, and currently is deciding how she is going to choose which among her many college admissions invitations she will take. By all outward measures, she is a success story.

But as a woman of color whose dress signals her faith, Maheera is regularly the target of abuse and insults in public. Too often she has heard the word *terrorist* muttered in her presence and told to "go back" to her own country (she was born in San Diego). She has been physically assaulted on public transportation and once had her headscarf torn off by a stranger who said he "needed to make sure she didn't have a bomb" (she was standing in line at a fast-food restaurant). "When I hear about a horrible tragedy somewhere in the world, first I pray for the lost lives, but then I pray that the criminal wasn't Muslim," she said. "When it is, I know things get a lot more terrible for me." When a mass shooting took place in a mosque, leaving dozens of worshippers dead, she said she felt numb. A woman on the bus told her, "That's what happens when you people go around blowing everything up." Maheera told us the story when she got to school. "There's so much hate," she said. "I don't understand. It's like some people don't even see me as human."

Maheera's chronic trauma stems from her identity as a Muslim in America in the 21st century. Born 2 years after the coordinated attack on 9/11 that took the lives of thousands of people, Maheera has only known a time when acts of open hostility routinely happen to her and members of her family. Her identity is complex, and the intersectionality of her race, gender, religion, and politics makes navigating young adulthood especially challenging. Her identity is strong—she knows who she is, and she likes herself. But her sense of agency is tested continually. "When something ugly happens, like an insult or something, I constantly have to think about how I will respond, or if I'll respond," she said. "It's all eyes on me when stuff happens, so I always have to look at myself from outside, too. If I defend myself, am I just fulfilling someone else's hateful beliefs about who they think I am?"

Maheera is facing stereotype threat, which has a debilitating influence on identity, agency, and learning. People face stereotype threat in situations when their identity, membership in a group, or affiliation with a group is viewed negatively. Fear of confirming a negative stereotype impairs one's ability to perform a task. Stereotype threat has one of the strongest negative influences on student learning, with an effect size of -0.33 (Hattie, 2018). This is a chronic form of trauma, most closely associated with gender, racial, and ethnic identities. Other affiliations also can be perceived negatively and contribute to lower expectations (foster children, homeless youth, and those who have a record of disciplinary actions are especially vulnerable to stereotype threat). Although not fully understood, it is likely that stress arousal is a trigger and sets off a cascade of behaviors and dispositions that, left unchecked, can result in performance well below the individual's capability. Long-term stereotype threat exposure can damage a person's beliefs about agency and identity.

IDENTITY AND AGENCY

Identity and agency form the core of who a person is and how they act upon their worlds. The social and emotional learning of children and adolescents is rooted in identity formation and agency. Theorists have discussed identity as a construct and as a set of crises that must be resolved in order to move to the next stage (e.g., Erikson, 1950). However, we will use a simpler definition: Identity is the story we tell ourselves and the world about ourselves. These stories include roles and are further informed by cultural, ethnic, gender, sexual, and national signifiers. Importantly, identity is a product of personality, dispositions, and experiences. Agency is about our actions, and our agency is rooted in our identity. Those with a high degree of agency believe that their actions lead to desired results, while those with limited agency feel helpless and ineffective. Beliefs about one's agency are linked to self-efficacy, which Bandura (1982) defines as personal judgment about the ability to reach a goal. Importantly, no one has a stable sense of agency across all experiences. Agency is situational. As healthy adults, we tend to construct our worlds such that we spend more time in situations where we feel a reasonable degree of agency, and we avoid those situations where we feel a lesser degree of agency. Children and adolescents don't have those options. Their situation is largely constructed by adults.

We believe that a primary outcome of schooling is the development of each student's identity and agency. Academic success is a not simply a metric of achievement; your academic success should influence your sense of agency. The more you know and are able to do, the more likely you are able to construct a world for yourself that capitalizes on your agency. Literacy is power, and it is currency. There is a reason that forced illiteracy has been used as a weapon against enslaved people. It is because reading and writing are dangerous. They equip those who are oppressed and marginalized with the subversive tools to change their destiny.

Young people who experience acute, chronic, or complex traumas are especially vulnerable to developing negative identities and a limited sense of agency. Further compounding this dilemma is that a traumatized person has a lower capacity to coordinate the necessary emotional and cognitive resources needed in order to learn (Holmes et al., 2018). The paradox is that while their academic learning is a potential key to building identity and agency, their traumatic experiences limit their ability to learn. We are reminded of Coleridge's (1834/1997) famous line of poetry: "Water, water everywhere/Nor any drop to drink." The opportunity to learn is present, but the ability to benefit from it is not.

As we have noted previously, experience is not destiny. A hope-filled school ensures that all students, and especially those who have experienced or currently are experiencing trauma, build their identity and agency. Schools that are trauma-sensitive have responsive structures that include specialized counseling and mental health supports. But it shouldn't start there. The social and emotional learning of our students begins in our classrooms.

SOCIAL AND EMOTIONAL LEARNING IN THE CLASSROOM

Whether intentional or not, we teach SEL every moment we are with students (Frey, Fisher, & Smith, 2019). Our interactions with them signal how others perceive them. The decisions we make model for our students how we resolve problems. Our reactions to them, especially when they are not their best selves, inform their understanding of the way people work through difficult situations.

The evidence about social and emotional learning is strong and has inspired educators to fold this approach into their curriculum. The definition of SEL as a constellation of skills, behaviors, and dispositions that define the holistic development of young people is widely attributed to the Collaborative for Academic, Social, and Emotional Learning (CASEL). Rather than residing in a separate space, SEL is understood as being a fundamental driver of academic learning (Mahoney, Durlak, & Weissberg, 2018; Waters & Sroufe, 1983). The influence on academic learning is substantial. Washoe County (NV) Public Schools reported that students who possessed high SEL competencies outperformed students with low SEL competencies by 20 points on the state's standards-based assessments of English language arts and mathematics (CASEL, 2017).

There are a number of models and programs that identify social and emotional learning competencies. We examined many of these models to locate how skills and dispositions clustered. We identified five tenets that move from the interior life of a child outward and extend to full community engagement:

> *Identity and agency* to foster self-confidence, self-efficacy, perseverance, and resilience
>
> *Emotional regulation* to identify emotions, manage stress, control impulses, and develop coping skills
>
> *Cognitive regulation* to manage attention, organization, metacognition, and decisionmaking
>
> *Social skills* to engage in teamwork; build, maintain, and repair relationships; communicate; and exhibit empathy
>
> *Public spirit* to engage in social justice and civic and ethical responsibility, exhibit courage, and lead (Frey et al., 2019)

But SEL efforts fail to reach their full promise when they are isolated from the consciousness of the school, staff, and community (Jones,

Bailey, Brush, & Kahn, 2018). There is a danger that SEL will become something that "we do on Friday mornings" rather than being woven into the milieu of the classroom. Far too often, social and emotional learning is delivered as a series of weekly preprogrammed lessons with little follow-through. The lessons are not customized to meet the needs and interests of the students being taught. And in some cases, they are used only in extracurricular programs such as those conducted after school. To be clear, there is much to be said about SEL in after-school programs, but not if there is a limited connection with the school day. These problems are exacerbated when adults are not a part of the equation. Jones et al. (2018) caution that indicators of poor program implementation include failing to consider the professional learning of staff. In addition, the researchers note that selecting an SEL program in the absence of input from key stakeholders, especially family and community members, is a mistake. Successful social and emotional learning requires an integrated approach within the academic curriculum and within the community.

INTEGRATING IDENTITY AND AGENCY

Students draw their sense of identity and agency in part from their experiences at school. One of the best ways for our students to explore identity and agency is by meeting fictional and real characters who must confront issues similar to those they themselves face. Picture books such as *I Like Me!* (Carlson, 1988) carry a positive message about self-confidence and invite students to make similar self-affirming statements about themselves. These should be contrasted with other literary experiences where characters must confront situations that compromise their identity and agency. Maheera, the student in the opening scenario, speaks fondly of the book *Does My Head Look Big in This?* (Abdel-Fattah, 2014) and the middle school teacher who introduced her to it. "The girl doesn't look like me, but I could so relate to it!" she recalled. Several years later, Maheera's sense of agency was on full display when she worked with fellow members of her school's Muslim Student Association to stage a live performance of the play version of the book for younger students at her school. "I want them to be able to embrace who they are and see the humor and love they have in their lives," she said. "That's what keeps you going. That, and knowing you're not alone."

Integrating Mindset

Students who have a diminished sense of identity and agency struggle to see themselves as capable of overcoming barriers to their learning. Much has been written about the importance of growth mindset (Dweck, 2007) and related behaviors of displaying grit and perseverance. A fixed mindset is evidenced in the belief that intelligence is innate and is not malleable. In other words, some people are "smart" and others are not. Consider for a moment that the outward behaviors associated with these dispositions are an outgrowth of identity. The nuances of fostering a growth mindset have been lost on some educators, who have misunderstood this as a product of cajoling students to "try again" and praising effort, rather than praising specific outcomes and decisions made together regarding next steps for continued growth and learning. One's mindset governs how challenges and obstacles are perceived, and the estimation of effort to undertake them. Mindset influences how feedback is received and whether the success of others is viewed as inspirational or a threat. There are several specific actions that teachers can take to develop positive, growth mindsets in their students. Dweck (2007) notes that teachers can use some fairly routine approaches to cultivate a growth mindset by providing students, especially those identified for additional support:

- Meaningful work
- Honest and helpful feedback
- Advice on future learning strategies
- Opportunities to revise their work and show their learning

There has been an explosion of general attention to growth mindset in classrooms. While we don't disagree that this attention is positive, the emerging evidence is that targeted intervention for students at academic risk is more effective. Sisk, Burgoyne, Sun, Bulter, and Macnamara (2018) performed a meta-analysis of 43 studies of growth mindset interventions for students deemed as being in need of further support. The researchers found that mindset interventions as a whole did not have much effect, although those that specifically involved students at high risk of academic failure (e.g., those who have failed a course) and those who live in poverty had a moderate influence on student learning. These interventions included regular meetings with students to provide feedback and examine their progress. In addition, effective interventions included reading about mindset, followed by reflective writing. Interestingly, the researchers noted that reading about mindset, without reflective writing, had little effect.

Students with adverse childhood experiences have a heightened risk of school failure and may be good candidates for growth mindset interventions and supports. These students often need assistance in identifying triggers that send them off in a negative direction. Talking through a challenging task with a student can help to interrupt this pattern. Stopping at a student's desk to engage in a quiet conversation about the student's prior knowledge regarding the task or about previous discouragement with similar assignments can spark their first attempt at resolving the problem.

Ellasyn is a student in Marta Camacho's 7th-grade math class and was identified by the grade-level team earlier in the year as someone who would benefit from support in developing a growth mindset. When Ellasyn read the first word problem on an assignment, she showed signs of distress. Ms. Camacho knelt down next to her desk and said, "Just tell me what you already know about this problem. I'll list what you say. Just like we've practiced."

Ellasyn thought aloud, while her teacher drew a T-chart on scratch paper. "Now tell me what math operation goes with each of the items you listed," said Ms. Camacho. As Ellasyn recited them, the teacher wrote the signs for the operations the student named. "Looks to me like you've got a plan for how to solve this problem," said Ms. Camacho. "Now give me two words to describe how you felt before, and how you feel now. Ellasyn said, *"Panicked* and *calmer,"* while Ms. Camacho wrote:

Panicked ➜ Calmer

"And what changed? What actions did you do take to change this?" asked the teacher. "I took a deep breath, and named the things I already knew," said the girl. Ms. Camacho made notes over the arrow. "You realize you did this, right? You had the answers, and I helped remind you about how to list it," said the teacher. "I'll bet you're proud of yourself for how you turned this around." Later, Ms. Camacho remarked, "Yes, it takes a bit more time to do that with Ellasyn, but what's the alternative? She needs tools that are going to carry her forward in life. We can't sit by. We can't afford to lose her." Ms. Camacho listed the successes she saw: Ellasyn was very much aware of her emotional response to the math task and, with the help of her teacher, was able to address the triggers and develop a plan for continuing to work through the challenge. "I don't just teach math," she offered. "I teach them how to use their power."

Understanding Triggers About Mindset

In addition to the perceived level of challenge, other common triggers include setbacks, overestimations of the effort required, reactions to feedback, and the success of others. We have all experienced setbacks, big and small. But for some people, these setbacks become roadblocks they can't get past. Being absent for several days due to illness is a setback, but a student with low beliefs about agency and mindset sees it as an insurmountable obstacle when they say, "Now I'll never catch up. I should just drop the class and try later."

The perceived amount of effort required also can be a trigger. Some people procrastinate when they believe that the amount of effort is significant. A person with a stronger sense of agency and identity schedules a time to focus on the task so that they can allocate sufficient time to ensure success. But for some, the amount of effort they perceive will be needed is the trigger that shifts them into a fixed mindset. Talking with the student to process what they can do, and to help them more accurately estimate what the task will require, assists them in making a plan.

Receiving feedback can be difficult for some students. After all, when others critique our work, we have to make a decision. We can use critiques from others constructively to improve our efforts and address mistakes, or we can see critiques as evidence that we don't have the skills and talents necessary to complete the task. Students prone to the latter may possess a lower self-concept and a fixed mindset that prevent them from using feedback constructively. English teacher Jacqueline Uribe uses an online peer editing and feedback system for her students to provide critiques of one another's work. Her students have been taught about responding to the writing of their peers, particularly to focus on specific aspects of writing for each task. The system masks the name of the person providing feedback, and Ms. Uribe has the system set to require that two students provide critiques of each submission. In addition, Ms. Uribe monitors the feedback to ensure that it is constructive.

When Abby received her feedback, she asked to meet with Ms. Uribe. Abby has struggled in the past in dealing with feedback. "There'd be a lot of pouting and hurt feelings at the beginning of the year," said the teacher. However, Ms. Uribe began meeting with Abby to process the peer critiques she received, as well as to discuss those the girl was writing for others. "These discussions really helped Abby," said Ms. Uribe. "When she would start to get defensive, I'd have her look back at her own. She saw that the feedback that she wrote to others was without malice. Wouldn't it be possible that the feedback from other people was also without malice? With practice, she began to realize that presuming good intentions helped her let go of some of her negative reactions."

Imagine how pleased Ms. Uribe was when Abby asked to check in with her a few months into the school year. Abby said, "This is the best critique I ever had. It's really specific and it tells me that there are parts that my readers really liked in my writing and a part that made them very confused. I re-read that part and I see what they're saying. I think I left out some details, but I can fix that. They also said that the voice changed, but I can't find that. Can you help? And, can I write a thank you note to them? Will you give it to the right people?" With practice and guidance, Abby has been able to recognize her triggers and manage them more positively.

Another trigger for some students is the success of others, or the perception that others are being more successful. It's human nature to compare ourselves with others and evaluate our success relative to others. But in many pursuits, comparisons with others are irrelevant. We are reminded of testing situations. As soon as the first person finishes, everyone notices. And if it is a student that peers perceive as "smart," this early finisher can trigger a fixed mindset in the students still taking the test. They compare themselves and feel that they are inferior based on the amount of time it is taking them to finish. Their teachers need to assure them that time is not the relevant variable in these types of assessments and that faster does not necessarily mean better. When teachers are clear about the problem with comparisons to others, they might be able to teach vulnerable students to avoid this trigger.

PEER RELATIONSHIPS AND SOCIAL CAPITAL

Most students will tell you the reason they go to school is to see their friends. As educators, we would love it if children said they go to school to learn about the world and to learn in the disciplines, but the truth is that peer relationships are an important motivator in school. For most children, peer relationships are generally positive and healthy, and when the small storms of short-term conflict arise, they have the tools they need to repair the relationships. But some students do not have strong peer relationships. Perhaps they move frequently and therefore don't have the opportunity to sustain friendships. Or they are hypervigilant and distrustful due to significant adverse childhood experiences. Therefore, they have a difficult time letting peers into their lives and isolate themselves from contact with others.

Positive peer relationships have a strong positive influence on learning. Positive peer influences have a strong effect size of 0.53, while feeling disliked by peers has a profound negative effect, at -0.19 (Hattie, 2018). Peers who encourage and comfort one another alter one's sense of identity and agency. But children and adolescents who are isolated are not able to draw on the protective factors of positive peer relationships. The peer relationships in the classroom impact the social cohesiveness of the learning environment and thus matter to us as teachers. Cohesiveness is "the sense that all (teachers and students) are working toward positive learning gains" and has an effect size of 0.44 (Hattie, 2009, p. 103). It is important to note that we are not speaking of friendships per se, but rather about the many varied ways that peers interact with one another during the school day.

Cohesiveness matters at the school level, too, as it is understood to be an important factor in the organizational social capital of the school. Organizational social capital is a measure of the resources and relationships a school community has to offer. The term draws on an economic connotation, as it is understood as the ways people in an organization invest in one another. At the school level, social capital is associated with graduation rates, academic outcomes, and school safety (e.g., Bryk & Schneider, 2002; Bryk, Sebring, Allensworth, Luppescu, & Easton, 2010).

Relationship networks offer another protective factor for students at risk. Hope-filled schools understand that investment in peer relationships is an essential part of the equation for supporting all students, and especially those who are at risk. Salloum, Goddard, and Larsen (2017) used a survey developed by Bryk et al. (2010) to identify four factors that predicted the social capital in high schools: normative behaviors, relational networks, trust in parents, and trust in students (see Figure 2.1). They found that social class was not predictive of social capital (well-resourced schools did not necessarily have a high degree of social capital). In addition, social capital is not equitably distributed (some students have more access to resources than other students in the same school). However, a school's social capital was

Figure 2.1. Social Capital Scale Items

	Strongly Disagree				Strongly Agree
Teachers in this school have frequent contact with parents	1 2 3 4 5 6				
Parental involvement supports learning here	1 2 3 4 5 6				
Community involvement facilitates learning here	1 2 3 4 5 6				
Parents in this school are reliable in their commitments	1 2 3 4 5 6				
Teachers in this school trust their students	1 2 3 4 5 6				
Students in this school can be counted on to do their work	1 2 3 4 5 6				
Students are caring toward one another	1 2 3 4 5 6				
Parents of students in this school encourage good habits of schooling	1 2 3 4 5 6				
Students respect others who get good grades	1 2 3 4 5 6				
The learning environment here is orderly and serious	1 2 3 4 5 6				

Source: "Social Capital in Schools: A Conceptual and Empirical Analysis of the Equity of Its Distribution and Relation to Academic Development," by S. Salloum, R. Goddard, & R. Larsen, 2017, *Teachers College Record, 119*, p. 12. Used with permission.

predictive of reading and math achievement and graduation rates. The researchers advised that "interventions designed to develop social capital in schools should be guided by deliberate efforts to strengthen access to school-based resources," especially connecting parents and community members to these efforts (Salloum et al., 2017, p. 20).

Peer relationships are an essential contributing factor to organizational social capital. Students who demonstrate care and respect for one another amplify the care and respect of the school's climate. Healthy peer relationships contribute to an orderly and serious learning environment. The classroom is an incubator for the development and maintenance of these relationships. But do you understand the social map of your classroom? A tool called a sociogram can help.

Use Sociograms to Identify Needs

A sociogram is a visual map of the relationships among people. Think of it as a way of seeing the social network in a classroom. Group dynamics shift over the course of a school year, and a sociogram is a way to take the temperature of the room. The purpose is to identify students who are marginalized and excluded so you can design responsive interventions to support them. A sociogram begins with data collection. Ask students to respond anonymously and confidentially to these four questions:

- Who are three people in this class you would most like to work with in a collaborative learning task?
- Who are three people in this class you would most like to play with at recess? (For older students, ask whom they would like to eat lunch with.)
- Who are three people in this class you would most like to work with in a collaborative learning task?
- Who are three people in this class you would most like to meet with for a fun weekend activity?

Note that students aren't being asked about current social habits, but rather about with whom they would like to interact. Tally the number of times each student is named and order them in concentric circles from most often to least often (Figure 2.2). The more times a student is nominated by peers, for any reason, the closer the student is to the center of the circle. Those who are rarely or never named are the most isolated students.

These data are useful in formulating heterogeneous groups in the classroom. The goal isn't to match those most frequently named to those who were not named, but rather to create table or work groups that represent a range of social networks, abilities, and identities. There is something to be said for proximity and shared experiences in expanding peer relationships in the classroom.

Use Class Meetings to Promote Dialogue

Brief whole-class gatherings held at regular intervals allow students to discuss topics and issues. As Potter and Davis (2003) note, their research showed that implementing class meetings three times a week for 8 weeks in their primary-age classroom "increased students' skills in relation to listening attentively, complimenting and appreciating others, showing respect for others, and building a sense of community" (p. 88). These class meetings are not used for conflict resolution, but rather for discussing matters openly. When class meetings are first

Figure 2.2. Sociogram Map

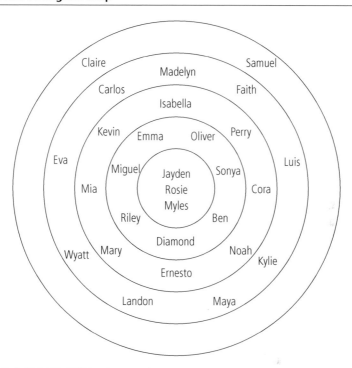

introduced to a group of students, the topics likely will be focused on the operation of the class. Over time, the topics generally expand to include the ways in which people treat one another. Typically, a meeting lasts 15–20 minutes and follows the agenda found in Figure 2.3 (Smith et al., 2015).

Figure 2.3. Class Meeting Agenda

- Call to order
- Encouragement pairs (students turn to someone seated next to them and offer a compliment)
- Old business (topics from the last class meeting that were not agreed upon or for which there was insufficient time)
- New business (topics that students want to discuss, often drawn from a box in which students have submitted topics either by name or anonymously)
- Shout-outs (students publicly thank, recognize, or compliment others)

Aid Students Who Have Difficult Peer Relations

Students who are marginalized often have a history of difficult peer relationships. These children lack the skills to repair and restore relationships and may engage in blaming others for their continued troubles. They may be hostile or physically or verbally aggressive, and thus deepen the level of peer rejection (Kim, 2003). They often lack the positive communication skills needed to forge friendships, including joining others in an activity, using positive nonverbal behaviors, and providing positive responses to others (Kim, 2003). Teachers can guide marginalized students by modeling and teaching these skills and brokering interactions until the students are able to develop friendships on their own. Teachers can do this by:

- Modeling appropriate ways to resolve conflict
- Encouraging fluid groups for projects
- Creating a safe community environment in the classroom

Teachers need to be aware that students who exhibit multiple aspects of a marginalized profile and prove resistant or unable to respond positively may require additional supports in and out of the classroom. These include modeling and feedback about prosocial behaviors, as well as specialized supports of the school counselor or social worker.

Children who have ongoing difficult relationships with peers require assistance in repairing relationships. This is more than simply telling two children to say they are sorry; they need tools for participating in conversations (e.g., ways to start a conversation or prompts to focus solely on the current situation), with a goal of making amends and moving forward. Restorative practices provide schools with these tools, offering a framework for repairing peer relationships, while equipping children and adolescents with the skills and dispositions needed for healthy human relationships.

Students who find themselves in conflict have difficulty reaching resolution without a system for doing so. Restorative conferences are conducted when harm has been done. Victims and perpetrators meet separately with a trained facilitator, and if both parties agree, a restorative conference is held. Depending on the circumstances, family members or friends may be invited to the conference. The facilitator uses a questioning protocol developed by Costello, Wachtel, and

Wachtel (2009) that poses the following questions to the person affected or harmed by the challenging behavior:

- What did you think about when you realized what happened?
- What impact has this had on you and others?
- What has been the hardest thing for you?
- What do you think needs to happen to make things right? (p. 16)

The child who has exhibited the challenging behavior is asked:

- What happened?
- What were you thinking about at the time?
- What have you thought about since?
- Who has been affected by what you have done? In what ways have they been affected?
- What do you think you might need to do to make things right? (p. 16)

The facilitator then engages those present and asks the victim what they would like to see as an outcome of the conference. The perpetrator also is asked how they would like to make amends, and when an agreement is reached, a contract between the two parties is created. It is important to note that restorative conferences do not supplant disciplinary actions and sometimes both are used together.

Eighth-grade student Joel's actions damaged the relationships he had with several peers and teachers. He felt that it was too much effort to repair them. During his restorative conference, Joel asked his parents whether he could transfer to a new school rather than work to regain the trust of his peers and teachers. He said, "It's just going to take too much time and work to make it right." But his parents understood the issue and said that they would support him in his efforts to rebuild because "it's the right thing to do, and you'll learn a lot about yourself in the process." The administrator in the meeting also offered to broker some of the interactions with teachers and peers by facilitating meetings so that the healing process could be sped up a bit and Joel could focus on restoring relationships. In the process, his identity changed from being "the bad kid" to one who is making strides. And his sense of agency grew as he saw that his efforts resulted in positive changes.

ADDRESSING BULLYING AND CYBERBULLYING

Bullying has a deleterious effect on the learning lives of children and adolescents (Schoeler, Duncan, Ploubidis, Cecil, & Pingault, 2018). Although not on the adverse childhood experiences questionnaire, bullying might be called an adverse schooling experience, as there are parallels to the effects of traumatic life events. Both have a dose–response effect, meaning that bullying experiences can cause a cumulative level of harm. In addition, bullying, like other ACE traumas, places children at higher risk of susceptibility to existing family challenges. Schoeler et al. (2018) note that "bullied children are more likely to be affected by personal and family risk factors for mental health, such as preexisting mental health vulnerabilities and socioeconomic and migration status" (p. 1230). Bullying is also predictive of future mental health issues. Their meta-analysis of 16 studies on the impact of bullying found that those victimized were likely to suffer from anxiety and depression as a result (Schoeler et al., 2018). The qualified good news, however, is that the longitudinal effect of bullying suggests that when the bullying stops, its negative effects taper off with time (Singham et al., 2017). Of course, counseling efforts can speed the effort.

A newer facet of bullying is cyberbullying of children through social media. Cyberbullying has arisen with the increased access to technologies by a larger number of children and adolescents. It is generational, too, as adults do not have similar experiences from their own childhood to draw upon. Unlike face-to-face bullying, cyberbullying is largely secretive and anonymous. Those who are victimized may not know the true identity of their tormentors. Even when they do, these acts usually occur in unsupervised spaces where adults are not able to intervene, and where bystanders who otherwise might defend a victim are less likely to emerge (Gardella, Fisher, & Teurbe-Tolon, 2017).

Wendy Ellison and her 7th-grade students had taken a field trip, but an incident of disrespectful talk on the bus marred the event. Three boys made disparaging comments about a girl's physical appearance, and while a few classmates had risen to her defense, most did not. The students directly involved in the incident, including the girl, met with Ms. Ellison and an administrator, and participated in a restorative conference that involved their families. However, the incident continued on social media, as other classmates joined in, continuing the drama away from the prying eyes of adults. Fortunately, the school had an anonymous reporting system, and administrators were able to intervene. But two issues needed to be addressed with the larger group. The first was the passive behavior of the bystanders who witnessed the incident but did nothing to stop the harassment in the first place. The second was the continued disrespectful talk among classmates that occurred on social media. While the perpetrators and the victim did not participate, many other students chimed in and made hurtful statements about one another.

Ms. Ellison's 7th-graders have a class meeting once or twice a week. It was Adrian's turn to serve as meeting moderator and he started by calling the meeting to order. After asking classmates to offer compliments or encouragement to a peer near them, he focused on a new item of business. Adrian began the discussion by revisiting the school's norms, which included a pledge to do no harm to self, others, and the school. "That means what we do online, too," he said. Ms. Ellison said, "A member of our class community was harmed. Did we honor our pledge?" she asked.

After an uncomfortable silence, Tyler quietly said, "We didn't do that." What followed was a discussion about peer pressure, bullying, and courage, with a recommitment to do better in the future. The teacher said near the end of the class meeting, "This was a low moment for us because we didn't behave like a family. But I can hear that you're learning from one another. We can put this behind us, but we can't ever forget the harm we caused by doing nothing, or by waiting until later to post insulting comments. Our inactions can be as damaging as our actions. Our actions on social media didn't match our values. Our words matter."

SUICIDE PREVENTION

Coauthor Doug recalls a time early in his career when a student attempted suicide while at school. During a faculty meeting that day, teachers were told by an administrator that Jessica had been depressed and wanted attention. The students at the school considered her "a lesbian punk." Doug said that none of faculty gave the situation much thought, and they returned to class the following day with no apparent plan for how to process the suicide attempt with students. He doubts that any of the teachers discussed this event with students, changed their lessons to address the topic of suicide, or thought about other students who were at increased risk for suicide. He recently had the opportunity to discuss this early-1990s event with a former colleague from the school. During their discussion, his former colleague said:

> I just went on with class. We were almost halfway through *To Kill a Mockingbird*, and I thought it better to focus on the book. I had heard that suicides can come in clusters and I really didn't want to talk about it, especially with students. I didn't really know how to talk about Jessica's situation, especially if her sexuality came up.

Our understanding of suicide has changed considerably in the nearly 3 decades since this event occurred. The Youth Risk Behavior Survey (2017) reports that over the 12 months prior to the survey, 7.4% of youth in grades 9–12 attempted suicide at least once and 17.2% of students had seriously considered attempting suicide. Females considered attempting suicide at a higher rate than males, 22.1% versus 11.9%. Suicide was the second leading cause of death for children ages 10–14, with the majority being males (National Institute of Mental Health, 2019). Schools are now understood to be a primary place for addressing suicide in general, being on the alert for suicidal ideations among vulnerable students, and intervening to marshal resources for students who are at risk for self-harm. According to the American Foundation for Suicide Prevention (2018), 27 states currently require annual suicide prevention training for all school personnel, and 12 states require formal written prevention, intervention, and post-vention policies. Fueled by the sobering statistic that suicide is the second leading cause of death for children ages 10–18, the Education Commission of the States (2018) reports that there are 10 legislative bills in eight states focused on suicide prevention in schools.

The integration of discussion about suicide into the classroom can build the resilience of students and aid in disclosure of suicidal ideation to a trusted adult. It is important to note that there is no evidence that talking about the subject of suicide or knowing someone who attempted or committed suicide increases suicide risk behavior (e.g., Kalafat, 2003). While there have been instances of suicide clusters, they are rare and are poorly understood (Niedzwiedz, Haw, Hawton, & Platt, 2014). This misconception is likely what prevented Doug's former colleagues from discussing the suicide attempt at their school and even now can be a cause of reluctance by educators to engage directly with the subject. However, three classroom practices can provide avenues for these essential discussions: young adult literature, student writing, and guest speakers (Fisher, 2005).

Young Adult Literature: "I'm Not Alone"

The value of literature as a means to address emotional needs of students is well known, and teachers are encouraged to choose selections that provide a mirror and a door for readers to understand themselves and others (Bishop, 1990). We will discuss the use of literature in more detail in Chapter 3; however, we would be remiss if we did not highlight the use of carefully selected texts in the context of discussing suicide. Many current young adult books deal with difficult topics in honest ways. Some teachers are shocked when they read these books because they are fairly explicit. One of our colleagues said, "I can't believe someone writes this—and for teenagers!" Having said that, our experience with these books suggests that students relate to them and respond to them in ways that invite their teachers into conversations about topics that matter. This is consistent with the view that literature response is a transaction between the reader and the text (e.g., Rosenblatt, 1978) and that readers make connections when they see themselves in books (e.g., Wilhelm & Smith, 1996).

Books that address issues related to suicide provide students with a sense that they are not alone. They give students an opportunity to interact with ideas and consider the consequences of suicide on the people around them. While general readings on suicide are important, teachers also can ensure that their students who are gay, lesbian, bisexual, transgender, or questioning have access to reading materials that let them know they are not alone. Remember that these students are at significantly increased risk for suicide attempts. These students often have difficulty establishing clubs in which to meet and discuss issues, as evidenced by the number of lawsuits across the country on the topic. Further, school personnel seem to have difficulty knowing how to address such issues. Many educators suggest that sexual-minority youth need positive role models (Blackburn, 2003; Henning-Stout, James, & Macintosh, 2000; Herr, 1999). Again, consistent with the idea that literature provides readers the opportunity to interact with people they may not meet and to visit places they may not see, it seems reasonable to suggest that classroom and school libraries should contain books that positively portray this segment of the human experience. Similar to the research on boys and the books they like to read (e.g., Smith & Wilhelm, 2004; Wilhelm, 2001), students who are gay, lesbian, bisexual, transgender, or questioning need access to books that engage them. An English teacher and colleague said, "Maybe if they read about a character who is gay and that person has a good life, they'll feel OK about their own feelings. I hope that books do that for kids—show them that they're not alone."

Providing students with access to quality books and the opportunity to read them is, and should be, a cornerstone of an adolescent literacy program (e.g., Ivey, 2002; Ivey & Broaddus, 2001). Students need time to find themselves in books, to meet people they would not be able to meet on their own, engage with ideas that challenge their thinking, and acquire new information. Adding books that address suicide and that portray sexual-minority youth positively is one way that educators can help with suicide prevention.

Student Writing: "Getting Inside Their Heads"

Student writing provides an opportunity for the teacher to understand students' perspectives, beliefs, and thinking. Students share their realities, and teachers have the opportunity to respond. But disclosures about suicide and other troubling topics can leave teachers feeling unsure of how to respond to student writing. Valentino (1996) classified the ways in which teachers respond to student writing into five categories:

- "Ostrich approach"—writing nothing in the margin
- "Rush Limbaugh approach"—noting errors in writing while ignoring the content
- "Sally Jessy Raphael approach"—inviting more information without helping by writing comments such as "thank you for sharing this with me"
- "Dr. Quinn approach"—wanting to do brain surgery when an open listener was all that was requested
- "Professional approach"—recognizing the pain ("This must have been a terrible experience") while offering help

Students with suicidal ideation need a professional approach that activates supports and intervention. Student writing allows teachers to identify a student at risk and to rally support around the student. In addition to responding to student writing and acknowledging the therapeutic effect that writing can have (Andrews, Clark, & Baird, 1997; Wright & Man, 2001), there is evidence that asking students to respond to the issue of suicide is appropriate. For example, Kovac and Range (2000) demonstrated that students who had lost someone to suicide benefited from writing about their thoughts, emotions, reactions, and experiences relating to this event.

Schoolwide writing prompts provide students with another avenue for developing social and emotional skills related to dealing with suicide and abuse. The American Psychiatric Association Alliance's essay project, "When Not to Keep a Secret," offers an excellent example of a schoolwide essay competition. Created to address school shootings, the national contest was designed to ensure that students knew it is OK, necessary in fact, to tell when they first hear about threats of violence. The essays allow students to reflect on their experiences in breaking a confidence and trusting an adult. Students often write about suicide, physical and sexual abuse, or self-mutilation in their essays. Writing can be a window into the world of young people and an important way that teachers can assist with suicide prevention initiatives. The vast majority of students tell someone, either verbally or in writing, before they attempt suicide. Further, warning signs often appear in the writing of students who are considering harming themselves.

Guest Speakers: "I See Red Flags"

Educators are not counselors or psychologists; it seems reasonable to suggest that these school- and community-based professionals be given access to adolescents on a planned, periodic basis. Many teachers invite guest speakers from the Yellow Ribbon Campaign (yellowribbon.org). Doug had the opportunity to participate in one of these sessions with a group of 33 9th-grade students. The guest speaker started the conversation with a discussion of the statistics on adolescent suicide and provided a note-taking form containing her major points for the students to use as she talked. For the first 15 minutes or so, the students appeared somewhat bored. In reality, they were more likely scared and unsure of whether they should participate in the conversation. When the speaker shared a personal story of losing a friend to suicide and the effect the suicide had on the people who were left, the class become exceptionally engaged. They asked a number of questions about why this person had committed suicide and what should be done if someone they knew was talking about suicide.

The guest speaker provided each student with an information packet on the risk signs for suicide. She also provided each student with what looked like a business card. Rather than providing her contact information, the card provided hotline information and instructions for asking for help, as well as instructions for a friend: stay with the person, listen, and get help. The students in the class were to give the card to someone they knew who was at risk for suicide. The cards are available from the Yellow Ribbon Campaign at yellow ribbon.org/cards.html, as is a template that can be used at no cost to print cards locally.

Before she left, the guest speaker asked the students in the class to write a letter to her explaining what her presentation had meant to them. She informed the class that she wouldn't read the letters until she was back in her office and would call the teacher or counselor if anyone asked for help. As the students finished their letters, the speaker asked them to seal the letters in envelopes and give them to her.

The following day, she called to inform the teacher that there were four "red flags" out of the 33 students in the class. Of the four, three reported a friend at school who was contemplating suicide, and one self-reported regularly thinking about killing himself. This triggered a suicide watch at the school and counseling services for students in need, as well as heightened awareness of the issue for students, teachers, parents, counselors, and administrators.

While guest speakers are not the answer for all students who may be considering suicide, they will increase the attention the school community pays to this issue. Teachers can be the ones who provide these trained professionals access to students so that they can begin the process of naming the issue, identifying students at risk, and initiating help for those who need it.

BUILD THE RESILIENCE OF STUDENTS THROUGH SOCIAL AND EMOTIONAL LEARNING

School occupies a significant portion of a child's life and should be understood as a crucial venue for the social and emotional learning of students. Yet too often school is viewed as a place for academic learning only. SEL runs the risk of being isolated from the mainstream of classroom learning. But what we teach in our classes holds the potential for serving as a rich platform for learning about the social and emotional learning necessary for student success. Hope-filled schools weave all these elements together in order to teach students about themselves, their power, and the ways they can keep themselves and others safe and away from harm. Children in hope-filled schools build their resilience, an important protective factor against trauma, and thrive in the face of other adversities. Some ways to promote SEL within classroom and school curriculum are as follows:

1. Identify social and emotional learning curricular approaches that fully involve the breadth of stakeholders in the school. Teachers, students, and other school-based adults should be involved in selecting and monitoring SEL initiatives, in consultation with families and community members. Training and data collection about its impact are vital in growing and maintaining an SEL initiative.

2. The content we teach offers many entry points for developing the social and emotional learning of students, especially those who have experienced trauma in their lives. However, commercial curriculum guides rarely call these opportunities out explicitly. As educators we often have to seek these out on our own. Conduct a curriculum audit to identify places in the curriculum that lend themselves to the integration of SEL.

3. Build the capacity of school-based adults to recognize the importance of identity and agency in the lives of children and adolescents. The language we use in our interactions should be humane and growth-producing, especially when a student is not being their best self. These efforts should be grounded in building a growth mindset and targeted to assist those students at risk academically and emotionally.

4. Invest in restorative practices to build the capacity of the school to teach positive social skills and aid students in repairing relationships that have been damaged. This is especially important for students who have faced adverse childhood experiences, as they may be hypervigilant and distrustful of others, and lack the communication skills needed to navigate the social landscape of youth.

5. Develop bully prevention and suicide prevention policies and practices if they are not already in place. If they have been developed, reinvest in the work of making sure that they are explicit, proactive, and revisited periodically across the school year.

Reflective Questions for You

- In what ways do I build each child's identity and agency with intention? What new efforts can I use to do so?
- Who are the students who display a negative sense of self? What do those children need to experience in order to change the narrative?
- Who are the marginalized students in my classroom? Am I aware of the social climate of my classroom?
- What communication processes do my students have in order to repair relationships? How do I assist those who struggle in this domain?
- Which students are at risk for bullying, either as perpetrators or victims?
- Does my school have a set of policies and processes for addressing cyberbullying?
- What do I need to learn in order to improve my suicide prevention skills?
- How do I keep reminding myself to not look away from a troubled student?

CHAPTER 3

Utilizing Literacies to Maximize Learning

Roxana, like many other high school seniors, is looking forward to graduation in a few months. Through a university–school partnership, her college prep English language arts class is participating in an online book club with local university undergraduates. Roxana and her peers first were provided an opportunity to view various young adult literature titles through a book pass and then selected a book to read. The plan was for undergraduate students to create questions related to story elements and prompts to enable personal connections with the text, and then share them on Flipgrid. High school students would interact with the college students in a virtual book club format, encouraging ongoing discussion while reading the novel. Roxana's English teacher moderated the virtual book club discussions.

Roxana is an average student who does not perform well on standardized assessments. Yet according to the Adolescent Motivation to Read Profile (Pitcher et al., 2007), Roxana highly values reading and perceives herself as a reader, with a strong desire to be able to choose her own books. Roxana grew up with her mother after her parents divorced. Her mother physically abused her for years, and it got much worse when she came out to her mother as a lesbian. After living in foster care for a few years, she now resides with her father, where she has been for a little over a year. For Roxana, school is her refuge. Books are her escape. She quickly signed up for this opportunity and chose the book *Burned* by Ellen Hopkins (2007).

Gracie, an undergraduate focusing on engineering, created general questions related to plot and character development, with the hope of building rapport and trust with Roxana and the five other book club students through their interactions. Roxana's beginning responses were short and did not provide a lot of textual analysis or personal information. She mainly related to the main character, Pattyn, and the fact that they were of similar age.

53

However, this changed as the group got further into the book. When they read about Pattyn's mother's continued abuse by her husband and decision to not speak out due to her religious beliefs, Gracie asked, "Why does her mother choose to stay in her situation?" Roxana used this space to open up about her own situation dealing with an alcoholic father who was abusive to her mother, connecting her own life to Pattyn's. Roxana stated, "I have been abused and so has my mother, in the past . . . [it is] embarrassing [because] your morale and confidence is just broken." Roxana discussed her frustration with Pattyn's mother and how she "just takes it . . . she doesn't do much, she's running away from her problems and sees it as her job to take it because that's what a good Mormon girl is supposed to do for her husband." Roxana explained that although this is a sensitive subject for her because of her own past, she appreciated the opportunity to talk about her life.

When Gracie and Roxana discussed how Bishop Crandall, Pattyn's family's religious figure, did not believe Pattyn about the abuse and disregarded her sexual orientation questions, Roxana emphasized how upset this made her. She told Gracie this was "mainly because I relate. That's probably what would have happened to me if I were in her situation . . . [as] I was raised in a very Southern Baptist home." Roxana continued by stating, "Someone who is LGBTQ, having one of your kids disowned, that's something I feared for a very long time. I remember coming out to my mom and she pulled out the Bible," telling her to read the passages stating that "man shall not lay with man and woman shall not lay with woman," and telling Roxana that she "was probably going to hell," as discussed in the book. The group discussed Roxana's question, "Why would somebody lie about that?"

Although Gracie could not directly relate her own experiences to those of Roxana or Pattyn, she often acknowledged Roxana and her feelings, displaying compassion and understanding. Gracie provided comments like, "It was really powerful that you shared something that's so sensitive and so close to you and such a personal experience. I really appreciated that. It definitely gave me a different insight into the book." Gracie also expressed the power of how Roxana could "connect books back to you" through discussions, even advocating for change.

This relationship continued to grow throughout the 3 weeks of reading, listening, discussing, and sharing together. Through interacting with Gracie and the book club group, and by relating to the characters and their experiences, Roxana demonstrated not only comprehension and critical thinking related to the novel, but also how this interaction with text provided an opportunity to discuss her experiences. Even after they finished the book, Gracie and Roxana continued to communicate, especially discussing Roxana's abuse. Roxana wanted to assure Gracie that she was now in a "safer situation" and appreciated talking about things.

Out of curiosity, Gracie asked Roxana why she was willing to share her own experiences. Roxana emphasized that it was difficult to openly discuss them with others but she felt that "people are being abused every single day and they don't say anything out of fear or they don't say anything out of embarrassment," like the mother in the book. Roxana stressed how reading books like *Burned* gave her a chance to grapple with abuse from the protagonist's perspective. Roxana said that it helped her realize that the abuse by her mother was not her fault. She accepted that "it is her issue and not mine." That healing occurs through discussion, identifying options and solutions, and then using one's own voice to make changes for oneself or others.

THE POWER OF LITERATURE

It can be easy to turn away from certain topics that cause tension or discomfort in our classrooms (Tatum, 2015)—topics such as drugs, alcohol, abuse, bullying, immigration, and many more, which are relevant and important to our students and their lives. But as one English teacher stated: "I feel strongly that we are confusing comfort with safety . . . I want my students to be safe. I don't want them to be comfortable" (Wolfsdorf, 2018, p. 42). Fortunately, children's books and young adult literature, whether narrative or informational, offer a means to discuss complex social issues, and especially how these events are compounded by societal issues about differences based on race, language, socioeconomic status, gender diversity, and disability. Through reading these texts, the "reader witnesses how the characters must adapt and adopt new modes of learning and communication even through challenges, hardship, and turmoil, which call for persistence, resilience, and self-affirmation" (Rodriguez, 2019, p. xvi). As noted earlier, tough topics need to be addressed in ways that are developmentally appropriate. But the sensitive introduction of such texts provides children and adolescents with a means to rehearse their responses, weigh options, and consider how they might use resources to affect the outcome.

IDENTITY AND LITERACY RESPONSE

Bishop (1990) discussed the need for students to have access to books that act as "mirrors" and "windows." As mirrors, books allow the reader to see herself through the actions, decisions, and dialogue of at least one character. Windows provide a way for a student to take meaning from the story, apply it to his own life, develop empathy, and gain knowledge about people unlike himself. As windows these narratives allow our students to meet people they otherwise might not have met. As mirrors they recognize the universality of human experience and let students know that they are not alone.

Rosenblatt's (1978) reader response theory posits that readers will approach, react, and understand a text differently, depending on the reader's cultural, personal, and social histories. The reader response approach is centered on the belief that students' reading and understanding of a text are dependent on the reader interacting and connecting with the text. Readers engage with a text based on their prior knowledge and personal experiences (Larson, 2009), and through discussion, students engage in meaningful, authentic connections with the text and one another. Therefore, readers create their own interpretations while they read and discuss, and they justify their reactions using textual evidence (Graves, Juel, Graves, & Dewitz, 2011), which in turn makes them feel that their perspectives are valued.

As an example of this theory, consider two students reading the same story about a young girl who stole food from the local grocery store because her family did not have money to purchase the food. If one student lives in a similar situation and can relate to the protagonist due to her own experiences with food insecurity, she may respond to the story through understanding and connecting. However, if the second student comes from a different background, a family that has never experienced food insecurity, this student may empathize with the story's main character but not be able to connect in the same way as the first student. Each will demonstrate a different response depending on how each fills in the gaps based on personal frames of reference. However, the textual experience and its accompanying discussion and writing are of great value for both students, even as their responses may differ.

Reader response theory transcends text types. In an age with a 24-hour news cycle and access to online platforms, students engage in reading of current events and similarly apply a lens that varies from one student to the next. Personal histories influence how the reader creates meaning, as does their prior knowledge of the topic. Troubling news events about violence locally or globally can be especially difficult to navigate, particularly in circumstances when a situation is evolving over a period of days or weeks. Whether fictional or factual, students are literacy consumers who need our guidance to come to terms with their responses. We can utilize literacy as a means to promote their strength, even when the circumstances are disturbing.

LITERACIES AS LEVERS TO MAXIMIZE LEARNING FOR TRAUMATIZED YOUTH

Our schools are filled with talented and diverse students who possess unique backgrounds, histories, and identities. They mirror a larger society filled with people of different races, ethnicities, family structures, sexual orientations, and socioeconomic classes. No student has a "perfect" life, completely free of challenges or obstacles. Negotiating these setbacks is an essential part of growing into adulthood. But a disturbing number, as noted previously, experience acute, chronic, or complex traumas that go well beyond the expected setbacks of growing up.

Although their stories of trauma are heartbreaking and disheartening, the good news is that we can make a difference. Literacy is a crucial tool for accomplishing the dual missions of teaching and healing. The literacy domains of reading, writing, speaking, listening, and viewing afford us avenues for building agency and identity, as well as resilience and coping. Think about it: As literacy educators we have some influence in determining the selection and use of texts. We can encourage meaningful and critical thinking, speaking, and listening through discussions that are undergirded with relevance. We can incorporate powerful writing assignments and activities that allow our students to reveal their dreams, explore their fears, and turn hope into action. Ultimately, we have the ability to choose instructional practices and materials that foster resistance and resilience. We can turn our classrooms into liberating spaces that allow students to ask questions, make decisions, and become aware of themselves and their ability to heal with others.

RELEVANCE AND TRIGGERS

It is important to note that although a main character may look like a student or may face a particular situation experienced by a student, this does not mean that students necessarily will find similarity between character and self. What is relevant to one person may not be relevant to another. Priniski, Hecht, and Harackiewicz (2018) conceptualize relevance across a continuum from least to most relevant.

> *Personal association* is through a connection to an object or memory, such as enjoying reading about travel because the student recalls riding in an airplane when she was younger. Personal association is the least meaningful on the relevance continuum.
>
> *Personal usefulness* is derived from a student's belief that a task or text will help him reach a personal goal. For example, a child reads articles about soccer because he wants to improve his passing skills.
>
> *Personal identification* is the most motivating type of relevance and stems from a deep understanding that the task or text aligns with one's identity.

Personal identification echoes the scholarly research on culturally relevant curriculum and its call for teaching and materials that reflect the racial and ethnic composition of our schools (e.g., Ladson-Billings, 1995). Identity-based motivation extends to the emerging research on *the possible other* as a form of personal identification (Oyserman, Terry, & Bybee, 2002), which acknowledges that people possess multiple identities that shift with the context. A student who finds *The Hate U Give* (Thomas, 2017), motorcycle magazines, and computer coding manuals equally fascinating may be exploring multiple aspects of identity rooted in past experience, present interests, and future aspirations.

We also need to be aware that some topics inadvertently could trigger memories or reactions. We are not advocates of trigger warnings per se, as there is little evidence of their effectiveness (van der Kolk, 2014). PET scan studies of people who had experienced trauma found that the neurological changes associated with recalling a traumatic event occurred whether a trigger warning preceded the memory or not (van der Kolk, 2014). We do agree with Wolfsdorf's (2018) assertion that as English teachers we are charged with introducing texts that "shake students from the comforts of their normative experiences, push them to reconsider their own ideologies, and—through significant, intelligent risk—bring about real changes in thought and experience" (p. 39). Having said that, texts should always be sensitively chosen with consideration of children's developmental level, especially their emotional and psychological lives. After all, there are many reasons why we don't teach *Lord of the Flies* (Golding, 1954/2003) to 2nd-graders. But confronting traumatic events through literature, both fiction and nonfiction, aids children and adolescents in processing trauma and creating a narrative space where such experiences can be discussed. Balaev (2008) notes, "Trauma, in the novel, lurches the protagonist into a profound inquisitive state, in which the meaning of the experience and the process of conceptualizing the self and world are meticulously evaluated" (p. 165). The vicarious experiences lived through protagonists equip students with insight about the event, and our making these texts available as options provides them comfort and acceptance in knowing that we won't turn away from their pain. Our failing to do so sends an unintended message of shame—that there are certain events we won't discuss. Our fear of addressing difficult subjects becomes their fear that they can't be loved. The teacher–student relationship discussed in Chapter 1 is vital not only to knowing your students well but also to addressing these concerns and issues when they arise.

It makes sense that books that feature protagonists of different races, cultures, or socioeconomic statuses provide opportunities for our students to relate to the characters, but students will also relate to books that feature protagonists unlike themselves who face distressing experiences. Through the eyes of the protagonist, our students get to see how these characters struggle through hardships, providing students the opportunity to relate to the characters and learn from them. Students even develop hope and healing for themselves if they have experienced similar terrible situations, or when they have grappled with a similar possibility. Perhaps most important, they can develop empathy for others in similar circumstances.

It has been said that the one literary device that frequently is used in books written for middle childhood is that the parent or caregiver is dispensed with in the first chapter. Whether through death (the *Harry Potter* series), travel to a different dimension (the *Wizard of Oz* series, *Alice in Wonderland*, *A Wrinkle in Time*), or just a convenient absence from the story line (*The Little Princess*, or almost anything by

Roald Dahl), young readers must confront a child's biggest fear: the loss of a parent. Reading can give them a place to safely navigate these emotions.

Older students are figuring out how to navigate a dangerous world that is riddled with uncertainty. For instance, our students may react in a myriad of ways while reading the part in *The Good Braider* by Terry Farish (2012) when a young male soldier is murdered for protecting the protagonist, Viola, from being raped by another, older soldier. Yet in spite of this, Viola continued to travel the streets to collect water to support her family. Her struggle to manage trauma and fear, while weighted with family responsibilities, speaks to the emotional struggles of teens who similarly must balance fears and obligations, or who also face dangerous people or situations in their own lives.

Another example of a high-quality text that explores a potentially daunting and controversial issue is *Out of My Mind* by Sharon Draper (2012), which addresses the intersectionality of bullying and disability. Bullying is prevalent in our schools, with around 25 to 33% of students having been bullied and around 30% of young people admitting to bullying others (stopbullying.gov). As noted in the previous chapter, bullying can lead to a negative self-image and even suicide (Centers for Disease Control and Prevention, 2014). Therefore, there is a strong need to include literature in our classrooms that discusses and deals with bullying.

Out of My Mind tells the story of Melody, a 5th-grader who has cerebral palsy. Although Melody does not speak and uses a wheelchair, her mind is active and bright, and she has a photographic memory. She enjoys things typical of kids her age: her family, music, and books. Melody is placed into a segregated classroom for students with disabilities. When she learns how to use a computer, she uses her thumbs to speak up and fight for placement in a general education 5th-grade class. Although she has lots of family support, she faces "mean girls," stereotypical assumptions and judgments, and limitations of school resources. Many of her classmates, and even some teachers, treat her as if she is stupid, insulting and mocking her, because of her style of communication. Ultimately, Melody, her community, and the reader come to understand that Melody's resolve to advocate for herself and others is an enviable strength.

This book provides not only a story of resistance and resilience but also a space to reconsider our own assumptions and prejudices regarding people with disabilities. As a student reads this novel, perhaps she will see herself in Melody or other characters. Perhaps she will begin to develop empathy for other students who are not exactly like her. Most of all, perhaps she will gain insight into her ethical responsibilities to stop bullying behaviors when she witnesses them. The relevance does not need to be confined strictly to personal association. It can have the potential of motivating students about personal usefulness and personal identification:

- Who am I now?
- What kind of person do I want to become?

Texts like these allow our students to understand that it is possible to persevere through acute, chronic, and complex traumatic experiences, while observing at a safe distance. Compelling characters like Viola and Melody allow our students to understand that they are not alone, that they have options, and that there is hope. Stories allow students to build protective factors such as resilience, problem-solving skills, resistance, and nondestructive coping mechanisms in their own lives, while simultaneously providing examples of how others confront and overcome traumatic events. Importantly, students develop social and emotional skills such as perspective-taking and advocating on behalf of others.

Teachers can provide supplemental informational texts that align with the topic addressed so that students can read and learn more about related themes and topics. For instance, after reading about Melody, a student may want to understand more about her disability. It is crucial to supply students with information about the resources available when an individual, family, or community suffers trauma.

Crucially, we do not want to communicate to students that they simply should accept current unjust realities. We want to empower them to use their voices to create constructive change. In their article "YAL as a Tool for Healing and Critical Consciousness: An International Perspective," Aziz, Wilder, and Mora (2019) explained how using a conscious stance gives both students and teachers an awareness of oppressions from internal and external forces, reminding students that their own worth is not determined by others. They present four guidelines for using young adult literature to "heal and raise student (and teacher) consciousness" (p. 75):

1. Adopt a conscious stance as a teacher. In other words, acknowledging the need for dialogue to support student awareness of internal and external struggles
2. Closely observe students' lives before selecting novels
3. Practice compassion—for the self and for students
4. Rethink the selection of texts beyond traditional milieus (p. 76)

With these guidelines, literature is used not solely as a tool for content instruction, but also as a means to understand through literature where those entry points for compassion and empathy exist.

USING DISCUSSION FOR ENGAGING AND ACTIVE DIALOGUE

When books are relevant to our students' lives, students are more likely to engage with them, leading to discussions and new understandings of important cultural and societal issues (Ivey & Johnston, 2013). Understanding that our students have experiences and backgrounds unique to their own situations also means recognizing that our students will read a text and take away their own interpretations. Students, including those who have histories of trauma, learn through collaboration (Crosby, Howell, & Thomas, 2018). Discussions about controversial texts and topics create a space where students can explore options for dealing with traumatic instances while resisting feelings of hopelessness.

SECONDARY TRAUMA AND DISCUSSION

Two traumatic experiences that students are exposed to are school shootings and the contentious political debate of immigration and deportation. The nearly universal trauma that students experience through their knowledge of school shooting events around the country, and by extension the threat of such an event that is present for any school, creates a secondary traumatic experience. Similarly, watching on television how children are getting ripped from a parent's arms while seeking asylum in the United States, and realizing that friends and loved ones also could be yanked from their homes, can create a secondary traumatic experience.

According to the National Child Traumatic Stress Network (n.d.), secondary trauma is the emotional duress that occurs from learning about a traumatic experience firsthand from someone else. Our students want to make sense of these experiences and process them with others. But too often, teachers do not feel comfortable and shut down the conversations. The good news is that we can change this by providing a space that encourages open discussions and questions regarding sensitive topics that students want to address. We can create classrooms and school cultures that promote conversations that develop and grow internal and external protective factors, such as good reasoning skills and civility (Henderson, 2013). These conversations may relate to current events or a student's specific situation that needs to be addressed, with optional solutions provided. Through dialogue, the classroom community provides students the ability to have a voice and be heard, and to build their capacity for empathy for others.

EMPATHY THROUGH READING AND DISCUSSION

A study conducted with 25 high school seniors found that using literature relevant to the lives of students aided in the development of empathetic responses from students because they were able to see themselves being placed in similar conflicts as the protagonists and they related to the characters on a personal level (Louie, 2005). Ivey and Johnston (2018) studied 8th-grade students' experiences of engaged reading with various texts. Students were actively engaged in reading when they entered "the social worlds of the narratives, and took up the perspectives of the characters, negotiating the problems they encountered, weighing difficult decisions, and experiencing characters' emotional-relational lives and the consequences of their decisions" (p. 144).

Teachers in these classrooms did not require all students to read the same book, did not set specific goals regarding the number of books to be read, and did not question students continually about what they read. Instead, the teachers provided room for students to choose books they wanted to read, books that were relevant to their lives or to the lives of other students of the same age, often containing moral dilemmas about race, gang-related violence, drug addiction, suicide, sexual exploitation, and teen pregnancy. Importantly, these teachers provided ample time for students to read with one another and discuss the books together. These were not highly structured discussions; instead, teachers allowed discussions to run their natural course.

The students' lives changed, and not just in school. Through conversations at home, with other teachers and peers, and with family members, students collaboratively grappled with their own feelings based on situations presented in the books, enhancing their own awareness of their relationships and circumstances. Literature became the means for students to release tensions and a forum to discuss issues that adolescents want and need to talk about but may be too scared or shy to bring up in class (Alsup, 2003). Ivey and Johnston (2018) identify the importance of allowing students to choose what they want to read and point out that tough issues do need to be discussed in class, spoken about straightforwardly, and not sensationalized.

USING DISCUSSION TOOLS

Discussion relating to texts may take place before, during, or after readings. For example, *This Is Where It Ends* by Marieke Nijkamp (2016) is told through the eyes of four different seniors (Autumn, Sylv, Tomas, and Claire). This fictional account chronologically reports the 54 minutes surrounding a school shooting. Through stories and reflections, the reader is forced to face bigger social forces in order to understand how a community can support or destroy a person who has endured various traumatic events.

Agree or Disagree

Prior to reading this text or a similar one, create an anticipation guide to spark pre-reading discussion that prompts students to explore their own attitudes and beliefs about the topic of the text. An anticipation guide is a list of a few statements that students are asked to agree or disagree with. The statements are related to themes, issues, or concepts from the reading selection and should allow for multiple perspectives and opinions. Statements in the anticipation guide should be discussed at various times throughout the novel, which provides students with the opportunity to reflect stable and shifting opinions. For instance, anticipation guide statements for *This Is Where It Ends* might include:

Agree or Disagree with the following:

- School shootings are preventable.
- One person can make a difference.
- Helping classmates in need should happen at all costs.
- Guns are the only threat to school safety.
- Most school shootings are due to bullying.

Another activity prior to reading is to ask students to select an image that illuminates and defines community for them. Students can discuss why they chose their image, what it means to them, and why it is important. The teacher then can begin a discussion about school shootings to provide space for questions prior to students reading the novel.

Circle of Viewpoints

Discussion should occur throughout the reading in order for students to stop and debrief. These discussions can occur either as a whole class or in small groups. Conversations can relate to the dynamic characters presented, their backgrounds that are provided through flashbacks, and their actions while enduring the traumatic experience. Circle of Viewpoints (Ritchart, Church, & Morrison, 2011) can be used to discuss actions through the eyes of selected characters. Students can be prompted to think about the text from the point of view of a particular character, responding to the following three discussion prompts:

- I am thinking of [an event, a topic, another character] from the point of view of [the selected character].
- I think . . .
- A question I have from this viewpoint is . . .

As the novel evolves, students return to the Circle of Viewpoints protocol, discussing how each of the major characters in the book perceives the events taking place in the story and explaining how each was treated by others and which characters exhibit empathy or resilience. After the novel is completed, students return to the anticipation guide and discuss how their thinking has remained the same or changed, and why.

Literature Circles

Another way to incorporate discussion within the classroom is through literature circles (Daniels, 2002). Literature circles are created when students are grouped to read, discuss, and possibly develop projects related to a single book, story, or poem. The discussion is student-centered as group members interact with the text together, engaging students in critical thinking and reflection as they read. There are different ways to incorporate literature circles within the classroom, with the most common having students read at home and discuss in class. The structure is especially useful for elementary and middle school students, who are still developing their discussion skills.

A selection of five to eight books, articles, or stories is presented to students. Through a book pass, students read the covers and flip through various pages of the books to rate their level of interest with each book option. Teachers then create small groups based on top options identified by the students, meaning that each group may read different books. Groups then meet on a regular and predictable schedule, taking on various rotating roles to engage the group while reading.

Daniels (2002) identifies various role options for students to take on to engage with the text and other group members. These roles are more formal at first to teach students about discussion and become more casual as the discourse becomes more well developed.

Discussion director provides questions to discuss with the group, ensuring discussion of the main points read.

Literary luminary highlights specific sections of the text that the group may want to read aloud or reread due to their being powerful, interesting, or important.

Illustrator creates a sketch, cartoon, or other visual to connect with the text personally or show the meaning of what was read.

Connector finds connections between the text and self, world (local community or globally), or other texts.

Summarizer provides the gist of what was read, emphasizing the key points.

Vocabulary enricher identifies words that either are problematic for themselves or could be problematic for other group members.

Travel tracker keeps track of setting changes through either drawing a map or diagram or keeping notes, including page numbers.

Investigator takes information presented in the book and finds additional, supplemental information to support an understanding of the background, places, or events discussed in the text.

The teacher is the facilitator as students exchange their own interpretations and questions, creating student independence, responsibility, ownership, and a sense of agency. The teacher should circulate around the room, listening in and interacting in discussions. It can be helpful for the teacher to model the literature circle process and roles with a whole-class reading of a short story.

Although traditionally an approach used for children, literature circles have been utilized to elicit critical literacies among adults. For example, Coleman-King and Groenke (2019) used literature circles to promote critical discourse of the book *Copper Sun* by Sharon Draper (2008) in order to help novice teachers understand that racism is not a thing of the past and to explore violence against Black girls and women. Through reading, extensive journaling, and discussions, small groups of preservice teachers found themselves thinking about what they had learned in school and questioning the history curricula of their past classrooms. This led to important discussions about what is included in history curricula, what is missing, and who is silenced. As a result, these teachers were better equipped to promote critical discussions in their own classrooms.

TEACHERS' RESPONSES AND DISCLOSURES

Classroom discussion can provoke difficult or discomforting moments for the teacher who is facilitating, especially when a student makes a controversial statement, discloses something troubling, or raises a question that requires a sensitive response. It is important to assess what information is needed in your response and to not make hasty assumptions. Gather information and learn about the situation. Share your own personal feelings of empathy, such as sadness, and keep the dialogue open-ended to allow students to express their concerns. Of course, it is important to know your students and their pasts before opening up sensitive conversations. However, it is impossible to know everything about them (Perry, 2014). Have a plan for students who unexpectedly get upset or uncomfortable to ensure that all students feel safe. Monitor discussions for a sense of unease from any student participating in the conversation, with an "out" plan for supporting students too uncomfortable to participate. And of course, keep your state's mandated reporter requirements in mind. Never promise a child in advance that you "won't tell anybody," as disclosures about abuse, neglect, and victimization must be reported.

WRITING AS CATHARSIS

Providing time for students to reflect on their own moments of trauma and to think about how that trauma impacts their own lives can be therapeutic. Bean (2005) suggests that the "integration of experiences" within curriculum becomes a "resource for dealing with problems, issues, and other situations, both personal and social, as they arise in the future" (p. 397). Wilder (2019) writes of an exercise called Conversations with Myself that provides space for students to first identify a difficult moment from their lives, isolate a specific segment, and then write a dialogue where their current self provides advice to their younger self. Specific exchanges are needed, namely a minimum of ten exchanges, including five from their former self and five from themselves at present.

The goal is to afford "an opportunity to reflect on their emotions surrounding a key experience and to identify a compassionate response that could have helped at the time" (p. 63). This has proved to be a therapeutic outlet for our students.

Another way to encourage writing to support healing is through private autobiographical writing, which allows students to write without interference. This space enables students to write about their experiences without having to openly discuss the details unless they want to invite other adults or peers to listen. This forum allows for personal reflections while students explore their circumstances, identity, choices, and possible connections with others if they share their writing. If a student wants to include the teacher or other students, this can be changed into a form of journaling where the teacher and student communicate with each other on paper or in digital form, providing the chance to think about what is included and decide how and what to share.

Writing poetry or a short story about personal experiences is also a great way for students to reflect on upsetting conditions. Teachers can use these authentic experiences during writer's conferences, focusing on specific standards and goals for writing improvement. This allows students to share their experiences while also addressing required objectives, such as writing narratives that are well developed, using sequencing, appropriate inclusion of details, and other writing techniques appropriate for the grade level. It is our responsibility to pay attention to what our students are writing and seek assistance if we notice a student mentioning traumatic experiences that need to be discussed with a school counselor.

STORY WRITING WITH YOUNG CHILDREN

As with text-based discussion, reading and writing can provide an outlet for students to relate what they read to their own personal situations. One way to incorporate writing with younger children is through group writing prior to and after reading a challenging picture book like *The Memory String* by Eve Bunting (2015). This tells the story of a young girl, Laura, who hasn't fully accepted her stepmother after losing her own mother 3 years earlier. To remember her mother, Laura keeps a memory string of attached buttons from personal and important family events, going back to her grandmother. After their family cat breaks the string, scattering buttons everywhere, Laura is upset about losing her mother's memories. Her father and stepmother look for a lost button while Laura is supposed to be sleeping. When her father attempts to replace the missing button with another, Jane, the stepmother, says, "It's like a mother. No substitute allowed" (p. 25). Laura hears this and realizes that Jane does not want to replace her mother, but wants them to be a family.

Prior to reading *The Memory String*, the teacher invites students to write a sentence or two regarding a time they lost a personal possession that was important to them. Then they read the picture book as a class, uninterrupted by discussion or questions. Then they read the story again, this time with students using sketch-to-stretch, a technique developed by Harste, Short, and Burke (1988). While reading, students draw their thoughts as Laura goes from sadness to despair to love. These sketches become discussion points with the class, as students share their drawings and explain their thinking about key details and events. Then the teacher moves the discussion into writing, inviting personal responses to the literature. Students can write about having a stepparent, write about something they keep that is precious to them, or reflect on how Laura shows personal growth and resilience by opening up her heart to Jane.

WRITING WITH ADOLESCENTS

Interacting and writing while reading literature are also appropriate for our older students. *The Border* by Steve Schafer (2017) is about a group of teenagers who flee Mexico due to devastating circumstances, seeking refuge in the United States. The story begins in Mexico, where Pato, the narrator, is attending his cousin's *quinceañera* with family and friends. The celebration quickly becomes tragedy when a local drug cartel interrupts the festivities, brutally attacking the attendees and killing everyone, even children. Luckily, Pato, Arbo, Marcos, and Gladys were off taking a walk. However, they quickly realize that the cartel is coming for them and a hefty monetary reward has been placed on each of them. They know that they cannot stay in Mexico and head for the United States with the help of Sr. Ortiz, an elderly man who watched his own children escape Mexico years before. As the four of them attempt to cross the desert, heading for the border, they realize that their guide is part of the gang that wants them dead. Throughout their trek, they encounter many difficulties, such as lack of food and severe dehydration, sickness, injuries, and the eventual death of one member of their group.

This young adult novel provides a different understanding of why people attempt to illegally enter the United States, disrupting the common stereotype that men and women are sneaking into the United States only to smuggle drugs or work illegally. Through reading and writing, students can reflect on their own assumptions about immigration and document their thoughts and reflections.

As students read, they can keep a journal of their thoughts, questions, and concerns, which may relate to gang-related violence or the loss of a family member or friend due to violence. They may record responses about Pato's near-death experience of almost running out of water while being lost in the desert. They may contemplate the need to leave one's only known home for the unknown. Students may wonder about the fears each character faces along the journey. They may even record their own experiences of loved ones who have entered the United States, or they may document how they would feel if either they or a family member were faced with this devastating situation. Through writing while they read, students can process their feelings and emotions.

When students finish reading, they can write poetic responses to allow them time to explore and express their understandings and feelings related to this novel. Poems can be structured or unstructured. Found poetry requires students to identify important ideas and feelings that were evoked as they read, using words and phrases taken directly from the text and arranged in new ways to share a different meaning. Haikus are another poetic option and require 17 syllables in three lines. The first line includes five syllables, the second line includes seven syllables, and the final line includes five syllables. Free verse poetry provides a little more freedom, as there are no requirements regarding meter, patterns, or rhyme. These poems can be used to relate to the characters, ruminate on personal feelings or relatable experiences, or extend questions left over after reading.

LOCATING APPROPRIATE LITERATURE
FOR READING, DISCUSSION, AND WRITING

Finding high-quality literature that explores these controversial issues can seem daunting. Traditionally, teachers have shied away from searching for texts relevant to students' lives, resulting in curriculum that perpetuates a single, dominant narrative that undermines the complex and variable experiences of our diverse student population (Nieto, 2018). Chimamanda Ngozi Adichie (2009) addressed what she calls "the danger of a single story." She tells about how growing up she felt pity for her "houseboy" and his family after being told he was very poor. She did not understand how his family was able to overcome hardships of poverty until she went to see the boy's village. She also shared how generalizations about her were made when she came to America to study at a university, with pity being the go-to emotion because she was from Nigeria—a place that consistently is viewed as a location of catastrophe. "But I must quickly add that I, too, am just as guilty in the question of the single story," Adichie says. She calls for people to not only know a single story but use a balanced approach, as stories can "be used to empower and to humanize" all of us.

Luckily, many high-quality narrative and informational texts have been published that can be included in classrooms and that are related to real-life situations that our students face. The International Literacy

Association provides three annual lists: children's choices, teachers' choices, and young adults' choices (literacyworldwide.org/get-resources /reading-lists). The Assembly on Literature for Adolescents of the National Council of Teachers of English (NCTE) has the annual Amelia Elizabeth Walden Book Award for Young Adult Fiction (alan-ya.org/ awards/walden-award) and various children's book awards, such as the Orbis Pictus Award, the Charlotte Huck Award, and an Award for Excellence in Poetry for Children (www2.ncte.org/blog/2018/11/2019-book-awards/). Additionally, NCTE has started various blog posts entitled Build Your Stack, with a goal of building teacher knowledge and book choices related to different topics, such as race, grief, and compassion (www2.ncte.org/blog/category/booklists).

There are many other award-winning works to peruse, depending on the preferred student-age group and topic. Some awards administered by the American Library Association are:

Schneider Family Book Award honors an author or illustrator for a book that embodies an artistic expression of the disability experience for child and adolescent audiences (ala.org/ awardsgrants/schneider-family-book-award).

Coretta Scott King Book Award honors outstanding African American authors and illustrators of books for children and young adults that demonstrate an appreciation of African American culture and universal human values (ala.org/rt/ emiert/cskbookawards).

Pura Belpré Award honors a Latinx writer and illustrator whose work best portrays, affirms, and celebrates the Latinx cultural experience in an outstanding work of literature for children and youth (ala.org/alsc/awardsgrants/bookmedia/ belpremedal).

Asian/Pacific American Award honors and recognizes individual work about Asian/Pacific Americans and their heritage, based on literary and artistic merit (apalaweb.org/awards/literature-awards).

Award for Excellence in Nonfiction for Young Adults honors the best nonfiction book published for young adults (ages 12–18) (ala.org/yalsa).

Additional notable awards include:

Indigenous Voices Awards support Indigenous literary production in its diversity and complexity, honoring the sovereignty of Indigenous creative voices while rejecting cultural appropriation (indigenousliterarystudies.org/-indigenous-voices-award)

High Plains Book Awards recognize authors and/or literary works that examine and reflect life on the High Plains of North America (highplainsbookawards.org/nominations-and-criteria)

American Indian Youth Literature Award honors writing and illustrations by and about Native Americans and Indigenous peoples of North America that present Indigenous North American peoples in the fullness of their humanity (ailanet.org/activities/american-indian-youth-literature-award)

The National Book Awards for Fiction, Nonfiction, Poetry, Translated Literature, and Young People's Literature (www.nationalbook.org)

BUILD THE RESILIENCE OF STUDENTS THROUGH LITERACIES

Trauma-sensitive practices coupled with student-centered curriculum and instruction build the capacity of young people to respond in healthy ways in troubling times. Through understanding and acknowledging the exceptionality of our students and their own cultural identities, we can use texts, collaborative and meaningful discussions, and writing to build children's and adolescents' resilience. We have the power to leverage literacies of reading, writing, speaking, listening, and viewing as tools that help children and youth navigate their lives.

Our students need educators who will stand up and protect them. Through interactions with teachers and other caring adults, including administrators and school and mental health counselors, students in hope-filled schools will make good choices and will seek answers for challenges and struggles. These types of conversations and relationships are important and something that we can all encourage.

There is a need to be cognizant when using books and literacy activities, as they may be triggers for traumatized youth and therefore should be approached with sensitivity. However, we advocate for the sensitive selection of texts that provoke meaningful discussion and writing, as these are tools for healing, self-acceptance, and empowerment. It is vital to have partnerships with the school counselor and psychologist to debrief from any instances or situations and discuss possible solutions.

Reflective Questions for You

The questions for this chapter ask you to reflect on your current use of reading, discussion, and writing in your own classroom. These questions are meant to encourage reflection but also to initiate goals for adapting instruction.

- How can I ensure that my classroom library includes multiple texts relating to various traumatic events?
- How can I choose literature for whole-group instruction, small-group instruction, and independent learning that supports the needs and experiences of all students?
- In what ways can I incorporate discussion to promote students' voices, allow individual interpretations, and make connections?
- Am I including writing opportunities to support resilience and resistance?

CHAPTER 4

Teaching for Empowerment

Middle school social studies teacher Bethany Morgan noticed that many of her students rarely spoke from their own perspectives, did not discuss their home lives or identities, and often sat quietly while they were taught history. Despite her efforts to draw them out, she had not been successful at establishing more than polite but superficial relationships with them. Then the burning of a local church rocked the small city where she taught. The police labeled the incident a hate crime, but the perpetrators had not been arrested. She overheard some of her students talking about their fear for themselves and their families. This teacher realized that her students might not feel safe bringing up these situations with adults, but that they did need a safe space in which to both explore their feelings related to this specific event and also understand other issues relating to their own community and cultural experiences.

After reflection on her required standards and course content, Ms. Morgan realized that her textbook included a unit on the topic of genocide, but provided a limited point of view, one that came from a dominant narrative and that did not foster questions or personal discovery. The curriculum was written by others and required students to sit, listen, and memorize. She reflected on how her students' experiences, perspectives, and identities were not included in the curriculum.

Ms. Morgan decided it was time for change that included a more inviting curriculum that represented her students. In addition, she wanted to provide her students with opportunities to investigate relevant experiences and events, noting that this offered an occasion to build student voice and agency. In particular, the teacher wanted her students to gain the skills needed in order to engage in historical thinking (Wineburg, 1999). She wanted them to understand that every primary and secondary source, such as historical documents, photographs, and news reports, included text, context, and subtext (Lesh, 2011). She wanted her students to discover multiple perspectives and to use them to inform their own interpretations and conclusions. And she wanted to provide her students with choice, which was lacking in her current curriculum. Ms. Morgan knew that memorizing facts and names was not the purpose of history instruction. The purpose of history was to ask compelling questions about human struggles over time.

She introduced the unit using the curriculum provided by the school, but this time her intention shifted. Now she was using her initial instruction as a platform for research and investigation on the topic of genocide. Through discussion, the class defined genocide as intentional harm, murder, or attempt to exterminate a group based on religion, race, sexual orientation, gender, country of origin, or ethnicity. As a class, they identified a desire to understand the influences that caused such hatred, with some students wanting to research their own family's experiences. For instance, one student from Syria expressed interest in researching her home country and her family's recent experiences as refugees. Several spoke of the genocide of Indigenous people in the United States during western expansion, which was the subject of Ms. Morgan's unit of study. As the class brainstormed ideas together, other students either identified their own familial situations or found topics mentioned by peers that they were interested in researching. At the end of that class period, the entire atmosphere in the class changed, with nine groups researching the required content of genocide but in ways that were relevant and of interest them.

Throughout the next few weeks, Ms. Morgan's students collaboratively researched their topics, found and analyzed credible and relevant sources, synthesized information, and shared their findings with classmates. They applied Wineburg's (1999) model for historical thinking, including close reading of primary source documents, contextualizing, and sourcing. Ms. Morgan invited students' families and other school faculty to attend presentations. Students shared their appreciation of Ms. Morgan for making instruction relevant in a unique and agentive way.

Although the teacher provided time and space for her students to research their own chosen topics, her instruction was aligned with the National Curriculum Standards for Social Studies. She took care to incorporate pieces of each of the 10 thematic strands, with emphases on culture and cultural diversity, interpretation and understanding of the past, individual development and identity, civic competence and agency, and the impact of global decisions and connections. Importantly, this was accomplished in a safe and inclusive environment.

LEARNER EMPOWERMENT AND ENGAGEMENT

Empowerment rests on the ability to mobilize resources to accomplish tasks and is an extension of one's agency. Learner empowerment is a key facet of motivation and fuels a student's sense of self-determination and decisionmaking (Brooks & Young, 2011). Thomas and Velthouse (1990) describe learner empowerment across four dimensions: meaningfulness, competence, impact, and choice. These conditions are crucial for human development, and their presence or absence influences the extent to which students engage. An essential practice of teaching is to foster a classroom milieu in which these conditions are present. However, a study of teacher preparation programs found that there is a dearth of instruction about motivation, belonging, and identity in learning, or what researchers Beaubien and Quay (2019) termed "psychologically attuned teaching" (p. 1). Much like Ms. Morgan, novice teachers often are left to figure out through trial and error how motivation and empowerment might increase student engagement.

Engagement is essential for reading, as it is associated with comprehension. Low levels of engagement and motivation make a difference in the reading achievement of upper elementary-aged students (Cho, Toste, Lee, & Ju, 2019). Gambrell (2011) characterized engaged readers as being "intrinsically motivated to read for a variety of personal goals, strategic in their reading behaviors, knowledgeable in their construction of new understandings from text, and socially interactive about the reading of text" (pp. 172–173). Consistent with Thomas and Velthouse's (1990) empowerment factors, meaningful reading tasks that provide choice are linked to improved reading achievement (Guthrie, Hoa, Wigfield, Tonks, Humenick, & Littles, 2007). Ms. Morgan further empowered her students by building their competence and sense of impact when she profiled their work through presentations to the school community.

Less well understood by educators is how students use meaningfulness, competence, impact, and choice in their own learning. We often think of these strictly as conditions we as teachers should create. But the reality is that students use these factors to make decisions about the task itself and the extent to which they will engage. In other words, students use these factors as an assessment to determine whether they will accept or reject the challenge. They might still participate at a minimal compliance level, but not engage in the deep learning potential.

When Students Feel Engaged and Empowered

- A task that is perceived by the student as:

being meaningful	"this work matters to me"
offering choice	"I have autonomy"

  is more likely to engage the learner.

- A task that provides the learner with:

an avenue for impact and influence	"I can make a difference"

  further increases motivation.

- A task that:

appeals to a sense of competence	"this work is worth my effort"

  empowers the learner.

EMPOWERMENT IS ACTION-ORIENTED

Empowerment thrives in environments where students are encouraged to take action. A hallmark of a hope-filled school is that it is action-oriented and possesses structures that facilitate empowerment. This is especially critical for students who have experienced adverse childhood events, as a loss of agency often accompanies traumatic events. Students who can recover a sense of agency are more likely to develop the resilience they need to overcome adversity (Henderson, 2013; Holmes et al., 2018; Masten et al., 1990).

A discussion of empowerment would be incomplete without attention to the essential role of teacher empowerment. Empowered teachers are themselves a conduit for empowering learners. As noted in Chapter 2, higher self-efficacy equates to confidence in taking on and working through difficult tasks. When teachers have a strong sense of their own instructional efficacy, they are able to create motivating, engaging, and empowered classrooms because they themselves feel empowered. In other words, teachers' sense of empowerment influences how they "structure academic activities in their classrooms and shape students' evaluations of their intellectual capabilities" (Bandura, 1997, p. 240).

Hope-filled schools organize themselves to provide the structures educators need in order to foster empowerment. Kanter (1993) developed a theory of structural empowerment in organizations. She asserted that structural conditions must be in place in order to empower members of an organization. These structural conditions include:

Access to support, including members internal to the
   organization, as well as outside agencies
Access to information that is timely, accurate, and relevant
Access to resources, including adequate funding of initiatives,
   materials, and personnel
Access to opportunities to advance one's learning

RELATIONAL CONDITIONS FOR EMPOWERMENT

The conditions necessary for teacher empowerment are not unlike those needed for learner empowerment in classrooms. While some of the details are different, the basic principles are the same. Kirk, Lewis, Brown, Karibo, and Park (2016) surveyed 381 high school students about their empowerment and associated classroom conditions. What they discovered should come as an affirmation that the work we collectively do matters. They used the Learner Empowerment Scale (see Figure 4.1), developed to align with Thomas and Velthouse's 1990 dimensions of empowerment: meaningfulness, impact, and competence (the fourth dimension—choice—was not a valid measurement on this tool). The researchers then compared the survey results with classroom and student factors to determine what might be predictive of learner empowerment. The quality of the teacher–student relationship was the strongest predictor. Students who had a strong sense of empowerment reported high levels of mutual trust, respect, authenticity, and understanding in their relationship with the teacher. The second strongest predictor was a classroom sense of community. Empowered students reported a heightened sense of membership, group identity, and relational connection to peers and the teacher. Gender, race, and parents' education levels were not predictive of learner empowerment (Kirk et al., 2016).

Figure 4.1. Learner Empowerment Scale

Please indicate in the space provided the degree to which each statement applies to you by marking whether you (1) strongly disagree, (2) disagree, (3) undecided, (4) agree, or (5) strongly agree.

1. _____ I have the power to make a difference in how things are done in this class.
2. _____ My participation is important to the success of this class.
3. _____ I can help others learn in this class.
4. _____ I can't influence what happens in this class. [R]
5. _____ My participation in this class makes no difference. [R]
6. _____ I can influence the teacher.
7. _____ The work that I did for the class is meaningful to me.
8. _____ The work that I did for the class is valuable to me.
9. _____ The things I learn in this class are useful.
10.___ The class will help me to achieve my goals in life.
11.___ The work I do in this class was a waste of my time. [R]
12.___ This class is not important to me. [R]
13.___ I felt that I could do the work assigned in the class well.
14.___ I can do well in this class.
15.___ I don't think that I can do the work in this class. [R]
16.___ I have what it takes to do well in this class.
17.___ I don't have confidence in my ability to do well in this class. [R]
18.___ I feel very competent in this class.

Source: Adapted from "Student Interest: A Two-Study Re-Examination of the Concept," by K. Weber, M. M. Martin, & J. L. Cayanus, 2005, *Communication Quarterly*, 53(1), p. 82. Used with permission.
Note to scorer: Items marked with [R] are reverse-scored.

CHOICE AND VOICE

If we are to empower students, we must provide opportunities for meaningful participation in activities that relate to their lives. At times, we need to take a step back from our already-created lessons and reflect on how what we teach can be taught using a student-centered pedagogy that fosters the kind of empowerment that is healing and that contributes to each student's resilience. It is up to us to determine whether we simply will tell our students what we want them to learn or whether we will engage them in personal discovery. The more we reflect on our curriculum and find ways to incorporate choice and student voice within our content, the more our students will learn about the world and themselves. Reflective thinking is in order as we check our own lessons to ensure that instruction connects to our students in meaningful ways. Marshall (2016) recommends asking the following questions:

- How does this lesson relate to the bigger picture of my discipline?
- How does it relate to other disciplines?
- Is there a connection to current events?
- How does it relate to my students? (p. 25)

If it is difficult to answer any of these questions, we must consider that either the lesson is more about the topic or concept as a "means to an end" or that the topic or concept itself may be too insignificant. We must equip students with the tools they need in order to ask complex questions, conduct research about topics that are relevant to them, and take action to improve their lives and the lives of others.

RESEARCH AND INQUIRY AS TOOLS FOR EMPOWERMENT

The saying goes that information is power. Students who are armed with the tools they need to think through problems, engage in inquiry, and locate accurate and factual information are able to speak truth to power. But if we limit the scope of what they read, and place a higher value on the passive consumption of information, we limit their possibilities. Instead of requiring all students to read the same text and respond in the same way, we can offer a more meaningful and purposeful type of learning. We can make the decision to engage our students in discussions to explore problems, questions, concerns, or challenges that they are facing and that are significant to their lives.

As an alternative to instruction that focuses on easy-to-answer questions or providing all knowledge through lecture, students can be given open-ended questions that require deeper, critical thinking, such as *what*, *how*, and *why*. We can inspire and boost students' creative nature by incorporating inquiry in our classrooms. Integral to inquiry-based learning are students who are active in their learning, collaborating with their peers "to formulate and address authentic questions of interest" (Savitz & Wallace, 2016, p. 92) based on "lived experience [that] connects this experience to the curriculum and guides students to address real-world issues in a consciously crafted classroom culture" (Wilhelm, Douglas, & Fry, 2014, p. 4). This type of learning is personal, meaningful, and differentiated, as groups and research are based on topic and interest, providing opportunities for heterogenous groups of learners representative of various reading and language acquisition levels (Irvin, Meltzer, & Dukes, 2007). In addition, inquiry-based learning can be used at any grade level and within any content area (Kerawalla et al., 2013; Levy, Thomas, Drago, & Rex, 2013). Many required standards for learning can be incorporated into inquiry-based learning (Harvey & Daniels, 2009).

Groundwork and Steps for Inquiry-Based Learning

To understand what this type of instruction may look like, we studied one teacher's use of inquiry-based learning in her intensive reading classroom (Savitz & Wallace, 2016). Samantha Harris understood that her students wanted to learn and in fact could read, but that they struggled with the required texts because of lack of interest or text complexity. She used the following seven steps to implement a unit using inquiry-based learning:

1. *Choosing a topic or theme:* Ms. Harris decided to use the theme of identity from her curriculum and textbook. She also thought about which standards would fit well within this unit to ensure that instruction was inclusive of them.
2. *Activating background knowledge and frontloading needed skills, concepts, and strategies:* Ms. Harris first brainstormed with her students as to what identity meant and then asked them to create "I Am" poems, writing about their own identities and beliefs. Some students shared how their identity related to their role in society, and others focused on specifics based on their race and ethnicity. Through sharing, her students created an environment of respect and safety, building a better sense of community. In addition, she built their conceptual understanding of identity at the surface level in order to equip them with the knowledge base they would need to engage in inquiry. It is essential to devote time to building foundational

knowledge, as inquiry that is not anchored in knowledge is ineffective (Fisher, Frey, & Hattie, 2016). Ms. Harris provided various texts on identity, such as articles on tribal identities and fingerprint identification. In addition, she introduced her students to short influential poems by Maya Angelou and Langston Hughes, and quotes from philosophers and scholars such as Martin Luther King Jr. After each was introduced, the students discussed their takeaways and thoughts, reflecting on and revising their evolving definition of identity.

3. *Discussing and identifying the conceptual and procedural goals:* As a class, they agreed that all groups would choose what to research and investigate, including forming groups, conducting research in class, and sharing their essential questions, research procedures, and information gathered related to their specific identity query. Ms. Harris led a discussion on options for their culminating project (e.g., live, video, or multimedia presentation; brochure; article to be shared with the community), with the understanding that groups could change their mind as they worked. .

4. *Discussing and creating open-ended essential questions:* With students already knowing the overarching topic and having read various texts relating to identity, the class created questions of interest, relating to either personal identities or societal issues. For example, one student wanted to research ways that body art can represent an individual's or a group's identity. Students formed their own groups, choosing from the essential questions presented and based on their interests.

5. *Conducting research:* Students worked together to locate and assess various texts and sources (e.g., poems, memoirs, novels, song lyrics, articles, and websites) that addressed their essential question. In groups, students supported one another with comprehension, synthesizing information, and vocabulary development.

6. *Teacher as facilitator:* While students worked in their groups, Ms. Harris was the facilitator. She circulated among the groups to encourage and monitor progress and ask questions. In addition, she used this time to provide small-group guided instruction using a gradual release of responsibility instructional framework (Fisher & Frey, 2014). For instance, she organized and worked with a small group of students who

needed additional support on determining bias and another group that struggled to find the main purpose of a source.

7. **Presenting the information:** After 2 weeks, each group presented their information to the class through various formats, some using traditional forms for presentations and others incorporating drama and art.

After presenting their findings, students reflected on their experiences. They were surprised by how much they had learned within their own investigation and from one another. They felt empowered, as they were "allowed to choose what they researched," which had been a rare experience for them in their education.

Inquiry in Content-Area Classrooms

In a math classroom, inquiry as a teaching method may be less familiar. However, Marshall (2013) suggests that math educators can "think about inquiry-based instruction as the strategies that unite the process standards (e.g., problem solving, representation) with the core content (e.g., proportional reasoning, graphing)" (p. 17). For instance, teachers may ask the following essential question: "How steep should a ramp be to allow wheelchair access?" (p. 59) Students then can use measurement to design a ramp and research to determine the height of the ramp. This process allows students to *do* math instead of only learning about math.

Perhaps no discipline is as closely associated with inquiry as science. Science classrooms already use the scientific method to form hypotheses and find evidence through data collection and experimentation to answer questions. Inquiry and hands-on experiences are vital for learning science and are included in the Next Generation Science Standards. As an example, one standard asks students to construct an explanation, based on evidence, for how the availability of natural resources, occurrence of natural hazards, and changes in climate have influenced human activity. Students can investigate how local communities adapt to and recover from natural catastrophes or how climate change impacts family farms.

High school students in chemistry teacher Angie Hackman's class embark on an extensive inquiry research project. They propose a topic for investigation to their teacher, then read scientific research journal articles about their topic. While the topic may include biology, psychology, or environmental science, an area of emphasis is an understanding of the underlying chemistry principles. Students develop presentations about their topic and share them at a showcase. Members of the school community are invited to the showcase, where the students answer questions about their topics and discuss them on an individual basis. Their choices are instructive and provide some insight into what these students care about. Topics from this year included:

- "Impact of Teen Depression on Social, Academic, and Physical Functioning"
- "Visible Tattoos in the Service Sector: A New Challenge to Recruitment and Selection"
- "Is Time Spent Playing Video Games Associated with Mental Health and Cognitive and Social Skills in Young Children?"
- "Cognitive Function Following Acute Sleep Restriction in Children Ages 10–14"

As Ms. Morgan noted at the beginning of this chapter, social studies is much more than presenting knowledge through lecture. The National Center for History in the Schools states that true historical understanding requires students to engage in historical thinking. Emphasis is placed on posing questions, acquiring credible evidence, and drawing conclusions from multiple sources and perspectives. These sources include primary source documents such as journals, diaries, artifacts, historic sites, works of art, quantitative data, and other evidence from the past (Herrenkohl & Cornelius, 2013). Students also identify the need to consider bias and subtext related to each source (Lesh, 2011).

One elementary social studies standard states that students are to understand family life now and long ago. Students can research the changing dynamics of family units, or the Great Migration, to understand reasons for movement across the country. Other students may be interested in understanding how families in different cultures interact and how they live. There are many ways to provide opportunity for personal choice and research, while addressing the standards and curriculum. It is important to note that scaffolding and extra support may be needed. Ways to support students include providing a range of additional resources for them to choose from, and customizing investigations to meet the individual needs of students.

At times, inquiry-based learning can be used to address and respond to schoolwide traumatic experiences, such as a violent incident or the death of a student. Schools can provide a safe space for students to ask questions, reflect on their own experiences, and research ways of moving past unexpected instances of violence or grief. Teachers may start this inquiry project by providing a space for open dialogue across the entire school or within classrooms. It is important to always address the norms and expectations of the inquiry project simultaneously, allowing students to choose their research topic related to the overarching theme or situation.

A hope-filled classroom provides students with ways to discuss, share, and learn together. Therefore, discussions and research interests may move in unexpected directions. The good thing is that there are many resources and websites that can provide students with useful and credible information to start their investigations. Although there are many valid, useful websites, here are six from reliable sources that represent varying topics related to adversity and resilience.

- RACE: The Power of an Illusion (pbs.org/race/000_General/000_00-Home.htm) is a website that aligns with California Newsreel's three-part documentary on race in society, science, and history. The site provides access to the documentary, along with additional resources relating to the developmental history of the social construct of race and makes visible how people experience race and discrimination differently (Demoiny, 2018).
- Facing History and Ourselves (facinghistory.org/) is a nonprofit international educational and professional organization that promotes the development of a more humane and knowledgeable society relating to issues of racism, religious intolerance, and hatred. It advocates for students to understand and connect history to their own lives to encourage greater ethical decisionmaking and understanding of their roles and responsibilities in a democratic society. The website provides various teacher resources for implementing discussion and debate in classrooms, fostering empathy and reflection of students.
- The Gay and Lesbian Alliance Against Defamation (glaad.org/) encourages dialogue about the difficult issues LGBTQ people endure, in the hope of shaping the narrative and accelerating

acceptance. In addition to the stand the organization makes through entertainment, news, and digital media outlets, various briefs and reports are provided, ranging in topics from acceptance of all people to specific instances of LGBTQ people in parts of this country.

- Kids as Self Advocates (fvkasa.org/index.php) is a national grassroots project created by youth with disabilities for youth. Members provide information and promote discussion based on their lived experiences, focusing on a Theory of Change. By attending public events and hearings, they offer voice and advocacy for youth with and without disabilities. In addition, they offer over 60 tip sheets and guides written by youth, for youth.

- Kids' Quest (cdc.gov/ncbddd/kids/index.html), part of the Centers for Disease Control and Prevention, offers interactive and entertaining ways to learn about health issues. Students first are asked to take a short quiz to determine prior knowledge, and to think about questions they may have, and then are provided with quick facts, additional websites and resources, movies, informational video clips, and books that can support learning. In addition, the website promotes further inquiry and investigation relating to the topic and the students' own school and community. Exposure to this site also gives students a resource for asking questions that they may be nervous addressing with their teachers or other school adults, such as about sexual health.

- stopbullying.gov is a federal governmental website that offers resources relating to bullying, cyberbullying, and prevention. The organization promotes conversations about bullying, with the aim of building a safe school environment through a community-wide bullying prevention plan. Resource information spans topics including specific policies and laws, research and support related to teen dating violence, disabilities and special needs, and prevention. Federal and nonfederal sources are available in the format of research, programs, fact sheets, infographics, and podcasts.

While inquiry-based learning provides students opportunities to research topics of interest to them, it is important to ensure that instruction is appropriately scaffolded, guided, and supported. This means consistently monitoring groupwork; providing graphic organizers or other scaffolds to support learning; engaging with each group through discussions, questions, and prompting to further learning; and modeling of strategies when first introduced. It is also important to note that while we want our students to think outside of the proverbial box of typical classroom pedagogy, we also need to be willing to accept differing opinions and multiple interpretations as students come to their own conclusions based on their own research and personal experiences (Herrenkohl & Cornelius, 2013). Through these types of caring relationships that honor and acknowledge our student diversity and diverse perspectives, we can provide protective factors that lead to our students overcoming adversity (Henderson, 2013).

THREE KINDS OF DEBATE OF CONTROVERSIAL TOPICS

Empowerment requires action, much of which is accomplished through communication and careful listening. Debate experiences provide students with opportunities to develop reasoning skills using accurate information. Argumentation skills are essential in disciplines such as science and mathematics, and are prominently featured in state standards.

According to the National Speech and Debate Association, there are seven types of tournament debate; however, three are more commonly incorporated in classroom instruction: Lincoln–Douglas, Policy, and Public Forum.

Lincoln–Douglas debates focus on logic, ethical values, philosophy, and questions of justice and morality, and position two individuals against each other. This type of debate includes a value structure where students demonstrate that the resolution, a statement or an assertion that places two sides in conflict, achieves or is in accordance with a value criterion. For example, "Resolved: A just school system should ensure instruction is taught in a manner for all to understand."

Policy debates focus on a specific local, national, or international proposed policy. This format concentrates on students' research, analytical, and delivery skills around current policy issues and perspectives from many disciplines (Cridland-Hughes, 2016). The affirmative side proposes a plan as the negative team simultaneously argues why the plan should not be adopted. This debate encourages the use of cards that include a tagline (the argument or claim), the citation of the source, and the evidence. Because policy debate relies heavily on direct statements of facts, paraphrasing is discouraged.

Public Forum debate topics are related to a current event. Although the Public Forum debate was developed as recently as 2002, it rapidly has become the most commonly used debate format in high school tournaments. Unlike Lincoln–Douglas debates, which are one-on-one, Public Forum debates are held between teams. They are notable for short rounds of 2–4 minutes, punctuated by several short crossfire rounds when both sides ask questions of each other. A judge moderates the proceedings and declares the winner. Students are prepared for both sides of the topic, as a coin flip determines which side they will argue. Fun fact: Ted Turner is credited with developing the Public Forum debate format, modeling it after *Crossfire* on CNN.

Although debate often is thought of as an outside-of-school tournament activity, the Urban Debate League (urbandebate.org) maintains that debate is meant not only for competition but also as a means to address social justice through advocacy. Debate provides a venue for our students to have a voice in matters that are important to them. Debate provides a sense of personal power and empowerment. In addition, there is potential for student debate to transform community beliefs, change traditions, and raise awareness. For instance, Littlefield (2001) surveyed 193 National Forensic League high school students, asking them to list three perceived benefits of debate participation. The most common responses were improved or increased

- communication and speaking skills—ability to speak in public
- knowledge and educational skills—knowledge of the topics and world and improved reading comprehension and writing
- collaboration with others
- research skills
- self-confidence and ability to be assertive
- analytical and critical thinking (p. 87)

While it does not appear on the League's list, being assigned defense of a position opposed to the student's own promotes learning and understanding of differing points of view and perspectives. An empowering education requires students to think critically, become social critics and agents of change, and take control of their own learning (Warner & Bruschke, 2001). Taking action also requires reflective and reflexive thinking. Reflection focuses on personal interactions following the action, and "reflexivity implies the abilities to reflect inward toward oneself as an inquirer; outward to the cultural, historical, linguistic, political, and other forces that shape everything about inquiry" (Sandelowski & Barroso, 2002, p. 216).

Cridland-Hughes (2012) explored how Robb, a high school student, felt about participating in City Debate, an after-school program associated with the League of City Debaters, a debate outreach affiliated with the National Urban Debate League network. Through the investigation of specific governmental policies, the program required students to apply their knowledge to inform action by exploring internal and external opportunities to learn about debate and to take on significant issues in their own lives and community, as well as national societal issues. Robb felt that City Debate provided a venue to not only organize and disseminate information relating to societal issues but also refine her ability to use text and knowledge to question decisions made by other people in power. She highlighted how she was able to not only reflect on the issues but also create steps toward making changes. She emphasized her growth in learning how to "cultivate relationships with peers whose beliefs differed from her" (p. 198). Prior to her debate involvement, Robb reported that she thought of only herself, her family, her community, and her school. However, after debate she realized that "other people have problems that are worse . . . but if it's somewhere else, then no one really cares about it" (p. 200). Her reflective understanding underscores the need for discussion of important topics that impact others globally.

Learning how to value differing opinions is essential for all our students. Teachers can incorporate debate in their classrooms, honoring student voice through debate speeches, while concurrently providing space for extension activities that are important in the community. There are additional ways to spur reflective thinking and encourage our students to think critically about controversial issues.

It is clear that these types of instruction encourage students to research well and understand multiple perspectives through critical and deep thinking and reflection relating to each argument. Often, debate involves controversial topics, such as immigration, homelessness, and other challenging events. Students may request specific debate topics and resolutions, or they may be provided. Debate encourages students to become more socially aware, engaged, and part of the community

Ways to Promote Thinking About Controversial Issues

- The Barometer asks students to think about their opinions on a specific controversial issue and then share them, by lining up with undecideds in the middle and others in a continuum based on their position on the issue.
- Another version of this is Four Corners, where students either strongly agree, agree, disagree, or strongly disagree on a statement, argument, or topic. In all cases, students explain their thoughts and opinions, providing various arguments or sides of the issue for the class to discuss. Students may go to a different corner based on what they hear from other students.
- Socratic Seminars are formal discussions that encourage students to co-construct meaning from texts through dialogic discussions relating to ideas, issues, and biases (Chisolm & Quillen, 2016; Israel, 2002). Through student-led collaboration, students listen attentively to peer comments, think critically for themselves, and articulate their own positions. Students learn how to find a common ground, with an emphasis on maintaining a safe and positive community through relationships with peers.
- SPAR (Spontaneous Argumentation) is a modified version of debate that requires students to speak from either an affirmative or a negative position on a previously discussed topic. This type of modified debate is much shorter in duration than a typical debate. Students are given 1 to 2 minutes to write down their arguments, followed by a 1-minute opening statement from the affirmative side. Students on the opposing side listen during this time and then present a 1-minute opening of their own. After opening statements, students are granted a short amount of time to prepare their arguments, followed by a 3-minute round to introduce new information or question opponents' reasoning and examples. To conclude this debate, students have a short time to prepare and then share their closing statements.

within and outside of classroom walls. When students learn how to support their own arguments, listen to opposing viewpoints, and react in a professional manner, they are less afraid to speak publicly and advocate at local and national forums (Warner & Bruschke, 2001).

Through collaboration, students ascertain new knowledge together as they work with their peers to accomplish a common goal.

CIVICS EDUCATION AND ENGAGEMENT

Civics education teaches students about their rights and obligations of citizenship at the school, local, state, national, and global levels. In addition, they learn about our nation as a democracy. Students are taught how to not passively accept the demands others place on them and to speak up for their rights, sharing in governance (Malin, 2011). Thomas Ehrlich (2000) defined civic engagement as making "a difference in the civic life of our communities and developing the combination of knowledge, skills, values, and motivation to make that difference" (p. vi). This requires students to be familiar with their rights and responsibilities, while also being reflective of their positionality as reflexive thinkers. Through informed action, students must be willing to use their voice and agency to address real public issues, impacting social change.

One example of incorporating civics at the school level is by posing a question or statement relating to school and community improvement for students to respond to. For instance, students may respond to statements like the following:

- "I would feel more involved in this school if . . . "
- "I am concerned about . . . "
- "I wish we could talk about . . . "
- "Something that would make me feel safer in this school is . . . "

These statements should be posed only if action is part of the plan. Few things are more frustrating than to be asked about concerns, with no follow-up. School leaders, faculty, and students should meet to discuss the results together and make decisions about future changes within the school.

Participatory civic skills are similar to those used in debate and inquiry. Students take their researched knowledge of a problem, engage in dialogue with those of differing perspectives, actively listen, and communicate their informed thoughts to promote actual changes that impact them and their communities. One way teachers can incorporate civic engagement within all classrooms is through discussion of current events. These topics can be identified either by the teacher or by the students, as students know what is relevant and important to their lives.

Service Learning

According to the National Youth Leadership Council (n.d.), "service-learning is an approach to teaching and learning in which students use academic knowledge and skills to address genuine community needs" connected to student interests. This means that service learning connects our instruction and curriculum with local, national, or global needs and priorities, showing students firsthand how our instruction affects real-world situations. Benefits include academic enhancement and increasing cultural and racial awareness (Baca & Lent, 2010). Service learning has a strong influence on academic learning, with an effect size of 0.54 (Hattie, 2018).

Service learning invites students to participate in important conversations that impact them and inspire them to get involved in bettering society. In addition, these opportunities cultivate caring relationships with adults within and outside of our classroom walls (Wilhelm & Novak, 2011). Together, students and community members build a partnership, a protective factor important for all students but especially for those at risk. Students spend ample time reflecting on their actions, their communication, their new knowledge, and their partnerships. A study of 51 students in a high school service-learning project found that participants scored higher on measures of autonomy, competence, and relatedness (connection to others) compared with before the project began (Kackar-Cam & Schmidt, 2014).

Service learning is not community service. One-off volunteer events, such as serving food at a homeless shelter on Thanksgiving or participating in a race for a charity, are personally rewarding, but they don't necessarily lead to academic learning. Boyle-Baise and Zevin (2013) explain that service learning is about "working with, not for" an organization (p. 217). Students need to understand that they can take what they are learning and apply it to real-world problems. The classroom link is the hallmark of service learning. Wihelm, Douglas, and Fry (2014) identify five types of service learning for students. Each type is needed and purposeful, as each provides student voice to advocate for changes, either for self, for community, or globally. They are:

Service to self: personal problem solving that leads to self-care and awareness and the development of personal empowerment (e.g., young children learn about nutrition, develop a shopping list for a healthy meal, shop for the ingredients with the teacher, and prepare the meal to enjoy as a class). This is a less common form of service learning, as the student is both provider and recipient of service.

Service to peers: inclusive, problem-solving experiences that value self, others, and everyone's experiences and perceptions (e.g., developing a set of fair rules with classmates about recess kickball games)

Service to school: small-scale version of the larger community where students can practice engaging in democratic actions and developing good habits of mind (e.g., setting up a school recycling program, developing a program and criteria for peer mediation services, or implementing a schoolwide mental health public awareness campaign

Service to community: application of student agency to participate in purposeful and democratic conversations, at the same time influencing positive changes in the community (e.g., working with a local animal rescue center to plan, promote, and coordinate a pet adoption event, or working with local community officials and organizations to provide protections and support for the homeless population)

Service to the environment and global community: students' empowerment and awareness that their knowledge and actions can better our world (e.g., working with a state park to survey plant biodiversity and creating a report for park staff, or using GPS to identify sites that need removal of invasive species)

It is important to understand that this type of learning does not happen overnight. Although some projects can be short-term, many take place over the course of weeks, months, or even the entire school year. *Teaching in the Cracks* (Schultz, 2017) offers detailed guidance about a variety of service-learning projects with a social justice orientation.

When organizing service-learning projects, it is important to plan ahead. Students may brainstorm ideas together, or specific opportunities may be identified by the teacher, school, or community. It is important to allow students to choose their projects and groups, based on their interests. Teachers also should provide a planning form that identifies the goal or purpose as well as a timeline of actions (i.e., steps, procedures, resources, consent), division of tasks by group member, acknowledgment of potential challenges, and plans for sharing what was learned (Lent, 2016). Class time should be dedicated for reflection, to allow students to connect what they are learning outside of school with what they are learning in school.

Action Civics

The National Action Civics Collaborative (NACC) promotes Action Civics, a youth-centered approach to civics education that addresses real-world problems. Per their website, the organization's mission is "to close the civic engagement gap by implementing Action Civics—student-centered, project-based high-quality civics education . . . [so] that all young people are prepared to be active and informed citizens." Their declaration on action civics is that it is not dependent on a specific content area of instruction; instead, there is a focus on the following four guiding commitments:

- Action, especially collective action
- Youth voice, including experiences, knowledge, concerns, and opinions
- Youth agency, including action, authority, and leadership
- Reflection, especially as it enriches the process (NACC, 2010, p. 3)

Gewertz (2019) reported how students in civics classes around the country have taken on the Action Civics framework. A group of 8th-grade students in Oklahoma were angry and felt misled about HIV and AIDS transmission and prevention. They realized that the information presented in the textbook, in keeping with a 1987 state law, was outdated and inaccurate. Further, it presented a negative perspective that stated that "gay or promiscuous people, intravenous drug users, and contaminated blood products were 'primarily responsible' for transmission of the virus" (Gewertz, 2019, p. 1).

Instead of letting it go, these students conducted their own research, invited guest speakers, and spoke with various political figures. Together, they drafted and submitted a new House Bill to replace the outdated language. It was through action that these students prompted a difference in their own education.

Action Civics takes the next step toward advocating change. Middle school students in Garden Grove, California, studied "the root causes of homelessness, identif[ied] the local government systems empowered to improve it, and research[ed] strategies that might bring about these improvements" (Gewertz, 2019, p. 4). These students spoke in front of the city council to advocate for building a new homeless shelter, after learning their city had only one existing shelter with 12 beds. Actions such as this allow students not only to have authentic audiences, but also to become personally involved in contributing to changes in real-world problems. This contribution and involvement while in school often lead to students staying invested in political and social engagement as adults (Watts & Flanagan, 2007).

BUILDING RESILIENCE THROUGH EMPOWERMENT

Today's society incorporates many modes of learning, including technology and digital media. When our students are faced with questions, they simply can turn to the Internet and find a gamut of answers. However, students may not know how to discern whether information is appropriate, valid, and reliable. In addition, our students need more from our lessons. There is a need to move away from simple memorization and restatement of facts and provide students with the means for conducting research, inquiring about topics, problem-solving issues, communicating findings, and being part of the process of change. Our students need to learn how to think critically, collaborate, and be creative (Partnership for 21st Century Skills, 2013). There is a need to step away from only thinking about what we need to teach and cover and instead make our instruction more intentional, focusing on what is important to us and our students (Marshall, 2016).

Part of being a teacher is being a change agent—"bearing witness to student learning, reflecting on it, and recognizing that student progress tells us something about ourselves" (Fisher, Frey, & Hattie, 2016, p. 131). Changing our instruction to be more student-centered than teacher-centered allows students to also become "insiders" within content and instruction (Lent & Voigt, 2019), a classroom practice in a hope-filled school. The best teaching "encourages students to develop the capacity to name the world for themselves, to identify the obstacles to their full humanity, and to have the courage to act upon whatever the known demands" (Ayers & Ayers, 2014, p. 13).

Reflective Questions for You

The questions for this chapter ask you to reflect on opportunities you provide for your students relating to research, inquiry, debate, civic engagement, and service learning. These questions are meant to encourage reflection but also to prompt inclusion of these needed forms of instruction within your own classroom.

- Am I providing opportunities for student choice that stem from their own interests?
- How can I better pique student interest and curiosity with my content?
- What would I need in order to incorporate inquiry-based learning or debate instead of lecture? Who are the students who would need additional scaffolding and support?
- How can I promote greater student agency in my instruction?
- Does my current instruction lend itself to civic engagement?
- How can I incorporate service learning opportunities for my students? What steps do I need to take to engage community partnerships?
- How will I monitor student empowerment opportunities to ensure that all students feel empowered?

CHAPTER 5

School Communities as Agents of Change

Nancy Johnson's 9th-grade English classes are not unique; they are similar to those in many high schools across the country. Her students witness violence in the community, and some likely contribute to the problem. She regularly has students who are on probation for crimes including gang fights, robbery, and auto theft.

While she wants students to learn to read and write well, Ms. Johnson also hopes that her class will help them understand themselves better. Throughout the course, she creates assignments that allow students to reflect on the questions of how their experiences influence their decisionmaking. During writer's workshop, Ms. Johnson confers with individuals about their experiences and alternatives to violence.

THE MASK PROJECT

One of the first assignments in the class is the Mask Project. Using a contour line drawing of a human face, Ms. Johnson has students draw a line down the center of the head, dividing the face into two equal parts. On one side they write "things people see," and on the other they write "things people don't see." Initially, students use the mask to analyze a character from a book they are reading. Once they understand the use of the mask, Ms. Johnson asks them to examine themselves. Tyneeia wrote about her personal mask and the things people see and don't see:

> I let people see a 14-year-old girl who always has a smile on her face and is always trying to make people feel good about them self and a really bad attitude because I take my sadness out on

other people. What I don't let people see is a 14-year-old girl who 50% of the time feels bad because the things my father says to me because he is drunk when he is not in jail and he come and visits. He will call me a bunch of names like ho or pig or bastard and that hurts me inside and he tells me he wish I was not his child and he only has one and that is my oldest sister. Then I have to go home and my mom's boyfriend is always starting things with my mom and I have to tell him to leave her alone and not hurt her. Sometimes I feel like I am 50.

Tyneeia had been a chronically troubled student in school, and this disclosure seemed to shed new light on the inner turmoil behind the aggressive attitude she exhibited. Yet Ms. Johnson knew that this student's writing could signal both an appeal for help and a warning to stay away. Such double messaging is not uncommon among adolescents coping with trauma (Dwyer, Osher, & Warger, 1998), and the teacher recognized that she needed to acknowledge the hurt without pressing for more details.

Ms. Johnson began a writing conference with Tyneeia by repeating the last line, "Sometimes I feel like I am 50." Repeating that line signaled her recognition of the girl's feelings. This simple technique of validating writing without trampling over the writer's words and emotions can effectively help students sort out their perspectives. Ms. Johnson did not make the mistake many well-meaning adults make in these situations—she did not begin by making a personal connection to her own life. Instead, by going to the heart of Tyneeia's theme and then waiting quietly, Ms. Johnson handed control back to Tyneeia— something many victims of violence crave. The subsequent conversations Ms. Johnson had with Tyneeia about her classroom behavior and school motivation resulted in Tyneeia's improved attendance as well as scheduled weekly visits to a school counselor. Through this assignment, Ms. Johnson was able to learn about this student's experiences and begin to help her address them proactively and positively.

COMPLEX TRAUMA REQUIRES COMPLEX RESPONSES

Christine Courtois (2004), a psychiatrist specializing in post-traumatic disorders, notes that "complex trauma generates complex reactions," as survivors bounce between re-experiencing and numbing (p. 412).

Tyneeia's conflicted writing is evidence of the internal duality she experiences. Some children marked by complex traumas live in households marred by domestic abuse and suffer chronic emotional damage. Others might experience complex trauma because of a stressed community's poverty, violence, and lack of a social safety net. The teacher's compassionate response is crucial, and while as educators we are not trained psychiatric professionals, we certainly can adopt a first-responder stance by ensuring that a child's first contact is a safe one.

But the community itself is an overlooked and underutilized resource for responding to trauma. Courtois reminds us that "having relationships with others and building support networks are crucial" for treatment and maintenance (p. 420). These networks can be found at the school level and within the larger community. Schools that are trauma-sensitive examine and revise policies and practices to support the needs of all children, regardless of whether they have had adverse childhood experiences or not. In fact, trauma-sensitive schools put systems into place proactively so that they can be responsive to the changing needs of students and families, such as loss of employment and homelessness. Given that a majority of school-aged children will experience at least one adverse childhood experience, why wouldn't we reorganize ourselves to be responsive to the emotional, social, and academic needs of students?

TRAUMA-SENSITIVE SCHOOLING

The terms *trauma-informed* and *trauma-sensitive* often are used interchangeably, but there are differences. According to the Substance Abuse and Mental Health Services Administration (2014), the term *trauma-informed* comes from the field of behavioral health and traditionally has been used to describe service delivery systems. Ideally, every school would have access to a broad array of mental health services. After all, school institutions often serve as a first point of contact for a child in distress. However, the term *trauma-sensitive* acknowledges that most schools occupy a narrower segment of mental health and social services, and have more limited capacity to deliver direct services. The Trauma and Learning Policy Initiative (TLPI) (n.d.), a joint project between Harvard Law School, Massachusetts Advocates for Children, and Lesley University, states that a trauma-sensitive school is a place in which all students feel safe, welcomed, and supported and where addressing trauma's impact on learning on a school-wide basis is at the center of its educational mission. The focus is on creating a whole-school culture that serves as a foundation for *all* students to learn and experience success at school. . . . The term "trauma-sensitive" helps emphasize that educators are not expected to take on the role of therapists. It also helps emphasize that, while behavioral health services will be an important part of the effort, helping traumatized children learn at school requires more—it also requires a school-wide culture that helps children feel safe and supported in all parts of the school. (emphasis in original)

To that end, we dedicate attention in this final chapter to developing and enhancing trauma-sensitive schools. This is the sphere of influence that most closely aligns with our collective power to enact change. It is understandable, looking across the landscape of traumatized students and families, that we quickly would become overwhelmed by the enormity of the task. The danger, of course, is to do *nothing* because doing *everything* is impossible. But we can do *something*, and it is significant. The first step is to become a trauma-sensitive school. In doing so, we can achieve a second goal, which is to build culturally sustaining alliances with families in order to contribute in material ways to the communities we are privileged to serve.

CHARACTERISTICS OF A TRAUMA-SENSITIVE SCHOOL

Have you had the experience of walking into a school you haven't been to before, yet you immediately gain a sense of the climate? As visitors, we usually first notice how we are greeted (or whether we are greeted). We notice whether adults and students make eye contact with us, and whether we are escorted to our destination or handed a map and told to use it to find our own way across campus. These are brief interactions, to be sure, but they speak volumes about the school climate. Notice that we didn't say school culture. The school's culture describes the policies and procedures that govern the school. But the climate is how it feels. Sometimes the school culture—the rules and norms—unintentionally communicates something else.

Take tardy slips as an example. Schools need to have a system in place to track attendance and tardiness. In many schools, students who arrive late go to an attendance office where they receive a tardy slip. "Why are you late?" a busy attendance clerk asks. At the school where two of us work, the approach is a bit different. Adults who don't have a first-period assignment are in the lobby, greeting late arrivals and telling them, "I'm glad you're here." There's still a tardy-slip process, but these adults know that this is a first point of contact for a student who may have had a difficult morning. It is an opportunity to put eyes on a student to get a quick sense of whether there is more going on below the surface. A student showing signs of something more serious than a wake-up alarm malfunction is ushered in to talk privately with a caring adult before going to class.

The school climate is the cornerstone of a trauma-sensitive school. There is a fundamental difference in an organization that seeks out problems, versus one that seeks out solutions. It is the difference between asking, "What happened to that student?" instead of the more common question, "What's wrong with that student?" A trauma-sensitive school is attuned to the needs of its children and seeks to find underlying causes that might be contributing to outward difficulties. Addressing the behavior in the absence of its source is analogous to firefighters fighting the smoke, not the fire (Family Resources, 2014).

A trauma-sensitive school infuses compassion and caring into each facet of the school. The policies, procedures, and climate are aligned to provide students with a safe haven for learning—something every child needs. The TLPI describes six attributes of trauma-sensitive schools:

1. Leadership and staff share an understanding of trauma's impacts on learning and the need for a school-wide approach.
2. The school supports all students to feel safe physically, socially, emotionally, and academically.
3. The school addresses students' needs in holistic ways, taking into account their relationships, self-regulation, academic competence, and physical and emotional well-being.
4. The school explicitly connects students to the school community and provides multiple opportunities to practice newly developing skills.
5. The school embraces teamwork and staff share responsibility for all students.
6. Leadership and staff anticipate and adapt to the ever-changing needs of students. (Cole et al., 2013, p. 18)

This is a vision, but without action, it will never become reality. The truth is that creating and maintaining a trauma-sensitive school requires rolling up one's sleeves and taking on the heavy lifting of transformation. What every school needs is the desire, of course, but also a plan.

A LOGIC MODEL FOR A TRAUMA-SENSITIVE SCHOOL

A logic model is a visual map for aligning activities with outcomes. A logic model consists of two major components: your intended work and your intended outcomes. Too often, initiatives are heavy on activities, but contain only a vague notion of what the intended outcomes will be. A logic model serves as a road map for a team and names resources, activities, outputs, and outcomes as necessary elements of a complex effort (W.K. Kellogg Foundation, 2004). Figure 5.1 is an adapted version of a logic model for trauma-sensitive schools that employs an evidence-based approach (Plumb, Bush, & Kersevich, 2016). The logic model is read from left to right, with an if/then statement linking one element to the next.

Resources (sometimes called inputs) are your assets. These include existing resources, as well as those needed to achieve the goals of the initiative. *If you have access to these resources,* *then these activities can be completed.*

Activities are the actions you will take to accomplish the goals. *If you successfully complete these activities,* *then these changes will occur as a direct result of the actions.*

Outputs occur as a direct result of the planned activities and are of benefit to your participants in the near term. *If the activities are carried out as designed,* *then these changes will result.*

Outcomes are the indirect and long-term results of the initiative, and impact other systems. *If participants benefit from our efforts,* *then other systems, organizations, or communities will change.*

A logic model is beneficial for complex initiative planning because it aids teams in examining the reasoning behind the actions they are considering. Importantly, this tool can highlight inconsistencies before implementation, allowing school teams to proactively address potential problems before they occur. Although a completed logic model

Figure 5.1. Trauma-Sensitive Schools Logic Model

Goal: Create a healthy school ecosystem that addresses the needs of each child.

Our intended work		Our intended results	
		Outputs *Direct Benefits*	**Outcomes** *Indirect Benefits*
Resources	**Activities**		
If we have access to these resources, then these activities can be completed.			
	If we successfully complete these activities, then these changes will occur as a direct result of the actions.		
		If the activities are carried out as designed, then these changes will result.	
			If participants benefit from our efforts, then other systems, organizations, or communities will change.
• Leadership team comprising key stakeholders • School-based mental health professionals with appropriate caseloads • Assessment tools • Support system within school • Social–emotional learning curriculum • Training materials	• Complete assessments • Analyze assessment results • Evaluate discipline policies • Create a plan to infuse trauma-sensitive practices into core programs and initiatives • Develop a school crisis plan • Educate staff on prevalence and impact of ACEs • Maximize caregiver capacity • Provide ongoing training on best practices	• Increased educational attainment • Decreased discipline referrals • Decreased suspension, expulsion, and dropout rates • Increased school attendance of students and staff • Increased social and emotional competence among students • Increased social and emotional competence among staff	• Improved school climate • Decreased intergenerational trauma • Improved mental and physical health outcomes • Fewer health-risk behaviors • Improved job satisfaction for staff • Decreased disability diagnoses • Improved social capital of the community

Source: Adapted from "Trauma-Sensitive Schools: An Evidence-Based Approach," by J. L. Plumb, K. A. Bush, & S. E. Kersevich, 2016, *School Social Work Journal, 40*(2), p. 60.

is read from left to right, its development does not follow that order. Use a backward-planning model to discuss the desired outputs (direct results) and outcomes (indirect results) so that activities and resources align in a logical and intentional way. Nor should this tool be used strictly as a quantitative assessment. Rather, the instrument is best used as a way to prompt discussion, collaboration, and action.

Resources

A trauma-sensitive school initiative begins with the creation of a leadership team that will guide the initiative, monitor progress, and make mid-course adjustments. This team should be multidisciplinary and representative of the key stakeholders. Recruit teachers, administrators, and school-based mental health professions, of course, but don't overlook the value of clerical and certificated representatives. Playground supervisors, cafeteria personnel, and bus drivers, to name a few, are vital as they see children in different contexts. Family and community representation provides the chance to extend these efforts beyond the schoolyard gate. Families are children's first teachers, and community members are critical for advising on the culturally sustaining focus of the initiative.

Assessment tools are needed for gathering data at the individual and group levels. This book features several assessment tools:

- ACE questionnaire
- Student–Teacher Relationship short form
- Social Capital Scale
- Classroom sociogram map
- Learner Empowerment Scale

In addition, Figure 5.2 shows the Trauma-Sensitive School Checklist, developed by Lesley University in partnership with TLPI. This checklist poses questions to school teams about schoolwide policies and practices, and classroom strategies and techniques. Importantly, this needs assessment challenges leadership teams to consider their linkages to mental health services, the extent of their family partnerships, and ties to community agencies. The work is extensive, and the intent is not to suggest that all of these categories must be addressed simultaneously. Rather, the results of the checklist give teams a decisionmaking mechanism for determining where efforts need to be focused and in what order.

Figure 5.2. Trauma-Sensitive School Checklist

A trauma-sensitive school is a safe and respectful environment that enables students to build caring relationships with adults and peers, self-regulate their emotions and behaviors, and succeed academically, while supporting their physical health and well-being.

This checklist is organized by five components involved in creating a trauma-sensitive school. Each component consists of several elements. Please assess your school on each element according to the scale:

1 = Not in place; 2 = Partially in place; 3 = Mostly in place; 4 = Fully in place

Schoolwide policies and practices

School contains predictable and safe environments (including classrooms, hallways, playgrounds, and school bus) that are attentive to transitions and sensory needs.

1   2   3   4

Leadership (including principal and/or superintendent) develops and implements a trauma-sensitive action plan, identifies barriers to progress, and evaluates success.

1   2   3   4

General and special educators consider the role that trauma may be playing in learning difficulties at school.

1   2   3   4

Discipline policies balance accountability with an understanding of trauma.

1   2   3   4

Support for staff is available on a regular basis, including supervision and/or consultation with a trauma expert, classroom observations, and opportunities for teamwork.

1   2   3   4

Opportunities exist for confidential discussion about students.

1   2   3   4

School participates in safety planning, including enforcement of court orders, transferring records safely, restricting access to student record information, and sensitive handling of reports of suspected incidents of abuse or neglect.

1   2   3   4

Ongoing professional development opportunities occur as determined by staff needs assessments.

1   2   3   4

Figure 5.2. Trauma-Sensitive School Checklist (continued)

Classroom strategies and techniques

Expectations are communicated in clear, concise, and positive ways, and goals for achievement of students affected by traumatic experiences are consistent with the rest of the class.

1   2   3   4

Students' strengths and interests are encouraged and incorporated.

1   2   3   4

Activities are structured in predictable and emotionally safe ways.

1   2   3   4

Opportunities exist for students to learn and practice regulation of emotions and modulation of behaviors.

1   2   3   4

Classrooms employ positive supports for behavior.

1   2   3   4

Information is presented and learning is assessed using multiple modes.

1   2   3   4

Opportunities exist for learning how to interact effectively with others.

1   2   3   4

Opportunities exist for learning how to plan and follow through on assignments.

1   2   3   4

Collaborations and linkages with mental health

Policies describe how, when, and where to refer families for mental health supports; and staff actively facilitate and follow through in supporting families' access to trauma-competent mental health services.

1   2   3   4

Access exists to trauma-competent services for prevention, early intervention, treatment, and crisis intervention.

1   2   3   4

Protocols exist for helping students' transition back to school from other placements.

1   2   3   4

Mental health services are linguistically appropriate and culturally competent.

1   2   3   4

Figure 5.2. Trauma-Sensitive School Checklist (continued)

Staff has regular opportunities for assistance from mental health providers in responding appropriately and confidentially to families.

1 2 3 4

Family partnerships

Staff uses a repertoire of skills to actively engage and build positive relationships with families.

1 2 3 4

Strategies to involve parents are tailored to meet individual family needs and include flexibility in selecting times and places for meetings, availability of interpreters, and translated materials.

1 2 3 4

All communications with and regarding families respect the bounds of confidentiality.

1 2 3 4

Community linkages

School develops and maintains ongoing partnerships with state human service agencies and with community-based agencies to facilitate access to resources.

1 2 3 4

When possible, school and community agencies leverage funding to increase the array of supports available.

1 2 3 4

Source: Lesley University, Center for Inclusive and Special Education and Trauma and Learning Policy Initiative, *a joint program of Massachusetts Advocates for Children and Harvard Law School.* Reprinted with permission.

Other needed resources include social and emotional learning curriculum for students, and accompanying training materials to support implementation by teachers. The Wallace Foundation has developed several resources to support teams as they design and implement an SEL-focused effort. These resources include a review of 25 leading SEL programs used in schools and by after-school providers, and recommendations for preparing for SEL implementation. These resources are located at wallacefoundation.org/knowledge-center/social-and-emotional-learning/pages/default.aspx. In addition, training in trauma, its prevalence and impact, and responses for children who have experienced adverse childhood experiences is critical. Take an inventory of existing resources and determine what might be needed.

Activities

The activities portion of a logic model represents the actions that your initiative will employ. This is the work plan and should align with the identified goals of the team. Early activities involve data-gathering and analysis, so the team can gain an accurate picture of current strengths and opportunities for growth. These activities also should include a comprehensive review of current policies and procedures that govern the school. One policy that may be in direct conflict with the team's desire to build a trauma-sensitive school is the discipline policy. While many states have enacted discipline policy updates that favor restorative practices over response-cost systems, others have been slow to do so. Review your current school discipline policy, as well as the de facto one that is enacted. Identify hotspots lurking under the surface.

- What are the racial, ethic, gender, and disability profiles of students who are suspended or disciplined?
- Among these students, who might be exhibiting maladaptive behaviors associated with trauma?
- Which teachers generate a higher than average number of referrals, and which do not?
- Are there zones in the school that are associated with higher discipline rates, such as the playground, lunch room, bus pick-up area, and gym locker rooms?

Ongoing training of staff and an ongoing program of orientation for new staff will be critical in implementing and sustaining such efforts. Awareness training is warranted at the early stages; professional learning should deepen the skills and practices of every adult, and must be job-specific. Classroom teachers, for instance, should be extensively involved in integrating social and emotional learning into their academic teaching (Frey et al., 2019). However, front office and clerical staff need training about detecting warning signs of trauma, responses when disclosures are made, and ways in which families and community members are made welcome (Fisher, Frey, & Pumpian, 2012). As the initiative matures, develop a plan for how new members of the school staff who were not present for the initial work will be onboarded as members of a trauma-sensitive school. Build the capacity of caregivers, including custodial grandparents, as an important part of this effort. Family and community membership on the leadership team provides invaluable insight into effective means for equipping caregivers with the tools they need to raise strong and resilient children. However, these efforts are likely to fail if they are culturally tone-deaf. Rather than adopting an approach that is a one-way transmission model that relies on telling parents how to improve, schools need initiatives that come from a place of respecting and working with families' perspectives and contributions. Parent empowerment efforts, supported by school and agency involvement, can result in lower parental stress levels, a contributor to adverse childhood conditions (Bode et al., 2016).

Outputs

The outputs in a logic model are the desired goals that are likely to result from the activities. These are vital to catalogue because they orient the team and other stakeholders to the work, and provide the team with a means to monitor progress and make needed adjustments. Common outputs in a trauma-sensitive school include a reduction in referral, suspension, and expulsion rates, and an increase in school attendance. These data are readily available at the school level and often are used as measures of effectiveness for many school-based initiatives. Trauma-sensitive schools monitor these indicators closely, and responsive systems are developed to support students and their families. Negative trends in these indicators are understood to be warning signs that a family may be in crisis.

However, less commonly monitored is staff attendance as a reflection of school climate. Higher rates of teacher absenteeism are associated with disempowerment and self-efficacy (Shapira-Lishchinsky & Tsemach, 2014). Compassion fatigue is an undesirable effect of working with traumatized people, and school leaders and staff are susceptible (Elliott, Elliott, & Spears, 2018). The secondary effects of exposure to trauma can leave caring educators with "lowered tolerance for frustration, an aversion to working with certain students, and decreased job satisfaction" (p. 29). Awareness of what compassion fatigue is, as well as active steps for addressing it, can be protective factors for adults. At the school where two of us work, a teacher proposed, designed, and implemented a mindfulness room for students and staff to use during school hours. He solicited feedback from others, proposed a budget, and met with the school leadership team to make it a reality. It rapidly has become a vital place in the school for people to restore their energy.

Outcomes

The outcomes section of a logic model describes the desired indirect benefits of an initiative. These outcomes may be more long-term, such as reductions in intergenerational trauma. Other outcomes may straddle direct and indirect benefits, such as the long-term effects of school-based health centers (SBHCs). Behavioral and physical health indicators often are closely associated and can impact school outcomes. As one example, there is an inverse relationship between childhood asthma and academic performance, as those with asthma miss more school and do less well on standards-based tests (Moonie, Sterling, Figgs, & Castro, 2008). Some communities, especially those located near freeways and industrial areas, experience rates of asthma that are far higher than national averages. Often overlooked is the fact that when children are home sick, a parent must miss work, with the loss of income further contributing to home-based stressors. School-based health centers can support children with asthma and their families to improve their physical health, reducing parents' work loss and increasing school attendance and achievement (Tai & Bame, 2011). These outcomes, in turn, positively influence outputs such as higher educational attainment due to improved academic performance. Our intention isn't to suggest that a trauma-sensitive school must include an SBHC. Rather, it is a reminder that supporting students and families in meaningful ways requires that we look beyond conventional school interventions. A growing number of schools in stressed communities have:

- installed laundry equipment for families to use
- partnered with local food banks to make nutritious foods available to families in need
- sponsored vaccination and wellness events

HOME-LIKE SCHOOLS BUILD RESILIENCE THROUGH CHANGE

"Home is not where you live, but where you are understood," observed German poet Christian Morgenstern in 1918. A hope-filled school is one that ensures that school is a bit more home-like, where children and families living in traumatized environments can find refuge and comfort. Throughout this book, we have spoken of resilience of individuals. But this chapter is really about the school as the unit of analysis. How might we build our resilience as an organization? It is not within our power to single-handedly eliminate all the causes of trauma. In a political landscape roiled by charges of racism, anti-immigrant biases, calls for violence, and acts of hate, it is understandable that we would lose hope in our ability to effect a positive change in the lives of young people. A trauma-sensitive school is a proven means for building resilience for children and families. But it is also how we co-construct a path toward our own resilience.

Critical education and critical literacy are two ways to do this. Critical education invites our students to take action when facing situations that require it (Shor, 1999). Critical literacy focuses on communities adopting a social justice orientation (Comber, 2015), using critical thought, knowledge, and action to create opportunities for advocacy. With one of the most debilitating side effects of trauma being loss of agency, critical education and critical literacy provide an opportunity to support student healing by providing spaces for students to have a voice and action.

But these are not just lessons to teach our children. We must fully embrace these messages of a social justice orientation as a guide for ourselves. We must see critical education and critical literacy as tools we use to build our own future. A hope-filled school is populated by people like you, who know we can establish pathways for our students to take back control. And in doing so, we save ourselves, too.

Reflective Questions for You

The questions for this chapter ask you to reflect on a systems approach to schooling in a traumatized environment. We draw on the works of Kolb (1984) and Moon (2004) to consider how to think systematically about how systems might be leveraged to support students, families, and ourselves. Their model of reflective thinking provides a clear line for decisionmaking and taking action.

- Noticing: What happened? Gather clear evidence and stand back from it to mull over what the data indicate. Invite others to locate patterns you may have overlooked. Remain open to alternative perspectives.
- Making sense: Do we have the information and skills we need? This is a gap analysis for oneself. Often the questions posed through noticing create a host of other questions that you are not yet equipped to address. This is a metacognitive stance that incorporates your own frame of reference into an event that can be changed.
- Working with meaning: What should we do next? Events exist in a social context that may influence a person's reaction to them. Consider the resources available and align them with the activities needed to accomplish desired outcomes.
- Transformational learning: How have our assumptions, understandings, values, and future actions been shaped by this experience? The work of creating a trauma-sensitive school impacts the lives of those it serves and those who are the agents of change. New ideas and insights should be formulated based on the results of the initiative. What has the organization learned because of this effort? Future actions should be discussed in light of these insights.

Literature Cited

Abdel-Fattah, R. (2014). *Does my head look big in this?* New York, NY: Scholastic.

Bunting, E. (2015). *The memory string.* New York, NY: Clarion Books.

Carlson, N. (1988). *I like me!* New York, NY: Viking Press.

Cisneros, S. (1991). *Woman hollering creek and other stories.* New York, NY: Vintage.

Coleridge, S. T. (1997). Rime of the ancient mariner. In W. Keath (Ed.), *The complete poems of Samuel Taylor Coleridge.* New York, NY: Penguin. (Original work published 1834)

Draper, S. (2008). *Copper sun.* New York, NY: Atheneum.

Draper, S. (2012). *Out of my mind.* New York, NY: Simon & Schuster.

Farish, T. (2012). *The good braider.* Las Vegas, NV: Skyscape.

Golding, W. (2003). *Lord of the flies.* New York, NY: Penguin. (Original work published 1954)

Hopkins, E. (2007). *Burned.* New York, NY: Margaret K. McElderry Books.

Nijkamp, M. (2016). *This is where it ends.* Naperville, IL: Sourcebooks.

Schafer, S. (2017). *The border.* Naperville, IL: Sourcebooks.

Thomas, A. (2017). *The hate u give.* New York, NY: Balzer + Bray HarperCollins.

References

Adichie, C. N. (2009, July). *The danger of a single story* [Video file]. Retrieved from ted.com/talks/chimamanda_adichie_the_danger_of_a_single_story/up-next?language=en

Alsup, J. (2003). Politicizing young adult literature: Reading Anderson's *Speak* as a critical text. *Journal of Adolescent & Adult Literacy, 47*(2), 158–166.

American Foundation for Suicide Prevention. (2018). State laws: Suicide prevention K-12. Retrieved from afsp.org/wp-content/uploads/2016/04/Suicide-Prevention-in-Schools-Issue-Brief.pdf

Andrews, J., Clark, D. J., & Baird, F. (1997). Therapeutic letter writing: Creating relational case notes. *The Family Journal, 5*(2), 149–158.

Ayers, R., & Ayers, W. (2014). *Teaching the taboo: Courage and imagination in the classroom* (2nd ed.). New York, NY: Teachers College Press.

Aziz, J., Wilder, P., & Mora, R. A. (2019). YAL as a tool for healing and critical consciousness: An international perspective. *The ALAN Review, 46*(2), 71–78.

Baca, J. S., & Lent, R. C. (2010). *Adolescents on the edge: Stories and lessons to transform learning.* Portsmouth, NH: Heinemann.

Balaev, M. (2008). Trends in literary trauma theory. *Mosaic: An Interdisciplinary Critical Journal, 41*(2), 149–165.

Bandura, A. (1982). Self-efficacy mechanism in human agency. *American Psychologist, 37*(2), 122–147.

Bandura, A. (1997). *Self-efficacy: The exercise of control* (2nd ed.). New York, NY: Freeman.

Bean, J. A. (2005). A special kind of unity. In E. R. Brown & K. J. Saltman (Eds.), *The critical middle school reader* (pp. 395–408). New York, NY: Routledge.

Beaubien, J., & Quay, L. (2019). *Training new teachers to understand motivation in the classroom: How teacher preparation programs are educating teachers on the pedagogical implications of the social psychology of motivation.* Mindset Scholars Network. Retrieved from mindsetscholarsnetwork.org/wp-content/uploads/2019/05/MSN-Teacher-Training-Formatted-Brief-v2.pdf

Benard, B. (2004). *Resiliency: What we have learned.* San Francisco, CA: WestEd.

Birch, S. H., & Ladd, G. W. (1997). The teacher-child relationship and children's early school adjustment. *Journal of School Psychology, 35*(1), 61–79.

Bishop, R. S. (1990). Mirrors, windows, and sliding glass doors. *Perspectives, 6*(3), ix–xi.

Blackburn, M. (2003). Exploring literacy performances and power dynamics at the loft: Queer youth reading the world and the word. *Research in the Teaching of English, 37,* 467–490.

Bode, A., George, M., Weist, M., Stephan, S., Lever, N., & Youngstrom, E. (2016). The impact of parent empowerment in children's mental health services on parenting stress. *Journal of Child & Family Studies, 25*(10), 3044–3055.

Boyle-Baise, M., & Zevin, J. (2013). *Young citizens of the world: Teaching elementary social studies through civic engagement.* New York, NY: Routledge.

Briggs, T. H. (1928). Sarcasm. *The School Review, 36*(9), 685–695.

Brooks, C. F., & Young, S. L. (2011). Are choice-making opportunities needed in the classroom? Using self-determination theory to consider student motivation and learner empowerment. *International Journal of Teaching and Learning in Higher Education, 23*(1), 48–59.

Bryk, A. S., & Schneider, B. (2002). *Trust in schools: A core resource for improvement.* New York, NY: Russell Sage Foundation.

Bryk, A. S., Sebring, P. B., Allensworth, E., Luppescu, S., & Easton, J. Q. (2010). *Organizing schools for improvement: Lessons from Chicago.* Chicago, IL: University of Chicago Press.

Centers for Disease Control and Prevention. (n.d.). Violence prevention: Adverse childhood experiences. Retrieved from cdc.gov/violenceprevention /childabuseandneglect/acestudy/index.html

Centers for Disease Control and Prevention. (2014). *The relationship between bullying and suicide: What we know and what it means for schools.* Chamblee, GA: Author. Retrieved from cdc.gov/violenceprevention/pdf/bullying -suicide-translation-final-a.pdf

Chisolm, J. S., & Quillen, B. (2016). Digitizing the fishbowl: An approach to dialogic discussion. *English Journal, 105*(3), 88–91.

Cho, E., Toste, J. R., Lee, M., & Ju, U. (2019). Motivational predictors of struggling readers' reading comprehension: The effects of mindset, achievement goals, and engagement. *Reading & Writing, 32*(5), 1219–1242.

Cole, S. F., Eisner, A., Gregory, M., & Ristuccia, J. (2013). *Helping traumatized children learn: Creating and advocating for trauma-sensitive schools.* Boston, MA: Massachusetts Advocates for Children.

Coleman-King, C., & Groenke, S. L. (2019). Teaching #BlackLivesMatter and #SayHerName: Interrogating historical violence against Black women in *Copper Sun.* In R. Ginsberg & W. Glenn (Eds.), *Engaging with multicultural YA literature in the secondary classrooms: Critical approaches to critical education* (pp. 122–131). New York, NY: Routledge.

Collaborative for Academic, Social and Emotional Learning. (2017). *Key implementation insights from the collaborating districts initiative.* Chicago, IL: Author. Retrieved from casel.org/wp-content/uploads/2017/06/CDI-Insights -Report-May.pdf

Comber, B. (2015). Critical literacy and social justice. *Journal of Adolescent & Adult Literacy, 58*(5), 362–367.

Cook, A., Spinazzola, J., Ford, J., Lanktree, C., Blaustein, M., Cloitre, M., & van der Kolk, B. (2005). Complex trauma. *Psychiatric Annals, 35*(5), 390–398.

Costello, B., Wachtel, J., & Wachtel, T. (2009). *The restorative practices handbook: For teachers, disciplinarians and administrators.* Bethlehem, PA: International Institute for Restorative Practices.

Courtois, C. (2004). Complex trauma, complex reactions: Assessment and treatment. *Psychotherapy: Theory, Research, Practice, Training, 41*(4), 412–425.

Cozolino, L. (2014). *The neuroscience of human relationships: Attachment and the developing social brain.* New York, NY: Norton.

Cridland-Hughes, S. (2012). Literacy as social action in City Debate. *Journal of Adolescent & Adult Literacy, 56*(3), 194–202.

Cridland-Hughes, S. (2016). Making words matter: Critical literacy, debate, and a pedagogy of dialogue. In K. A. Davis, M.L.W. Zorwick, J. Roland, & M. M. Wade (Eds.), *Using debate in the classroom: Encouraging critical thinking, communication, and collaboration* (pp. 48–59). New York, NY: Routledge.

Crosby, S. D., Howell, P., & Thomas, S. (2018). Social justice education through trauma-informed teaching. *Middle School Journal, 49*(4), 15–23.

Daniels, H. (2002). *Literature circles: Voice and choice in book clubs and reading groups* (2nd ed.). Portsmouth, NH: Stenhouse.

Demoiny, S. B. (2018). Websites to explore race as a social construct. *Journal of Adolescent & Adult Literacy, 61*(4), 469–472.

Demorest, A., Meyer, C., Phelps, E., Gardner, H., & Winner, E. (1984). Words speak louder than actions: Understanding deliberately false remarks. *Child Development, 55*, 1527–1534.

Dews, S., & Winner, E. (1995). Muting the meaning: A social function of irony. *Metaphor and Symbolic Activity, 10*, 3–18.

Dweck, C. (2007). *Growth mindset: The new psychology of success.* New York, NY: Ballantine.

Dwyer, K., Osher, D., & Warger, C. (1998). *Early warning, timely response: A guide to safe schools.* Washington, DC: U.S. Department of Education.

Education Commission of the States. (2018, September 17). *Suicide prevention in schools: What are states doing to prevent youth suicide?* Retrieved from ednote.ecs.org/suicide-prevention-in-schools-what-are-states-doing-to-prevent-youth-suicide/

Ehrlich, T. (2000). *Civics responsibility and higher education.* Westport, CT: American Council on Education/Oryx Press.

Elliott, K. W., Elliott, J. K., & Spears, S. G. (2018). Teaching on empty. *Principal, 98*(2), 28–29.

Erikson, E. H. (1950). *Childhood and society.* New York, NY: Norton.

Family Resources. (2014). *Trauma and violence exposure.* Davenport, IA: Quad Cities Trauma Consortium.

Felitti, V. J., Anda, R. F., Nordenberg, D., Williamson, D. F., Spitz, A. M., Edwards, V., . . . Marks, J. S. (1998). Relationship of childhood abuse and household dysfunction to many of the leading causes of death in adults. *American Journal of Preventive Medicine, 14*(4), 245–258.

Finkelhor, D., Ormrod, R. K., & Turner, H. A. (2007). Poly-victimization: A neglected component in child victimization. *Child Abuse & Neglect, 31*(1), 7–26.

Fisher, D. (2005). The literacy educator's role in suicide prevention. *Journal of Adolescent & Adult Literacy, 48*(5), 364–373.

Fisher, D., & Frey, N. (2014). *Better learning through structure teaching: A framework for the gradual release of responsibility* (2nd ed.). Alexandria, VA: ASCD.

Fisher, D., Frey, N., & Hattie, J. (2016). *Visible learning for literacy: Implementing the practices that work best to accelerate student learning.* Thousand Oaks, CA: Corwin.

Fisher, D., Frey, N., & Pumpian, I. (2012). *How to create a culture of achievement in your school and classroom.* Alexandria, VA: Association for Supervision and Curriculum Development.

Frey, N., & Fisher, D. (2008). The under-appreciated role of humiliation in the middle school. *Middle School Journal, 39*(3), 4–12.

Frey, N., Fisher, D., & Smith, D. (2019). *All learning is social and emotional: Helping students develop essential skills for the classroom and beyond.* Alexandria, VA: Association for Supervision and Curriculum Development.

Friedman, T. L. (2005). *The world is flat: A brief history of the twenty-first century.* New York, NY: Farrar, Straus and Giroux.

Gambrell, L. (2011). Seven rules of engagement: What's most important to know about motivation to read. *The Reading Teacher, 65*(3), 172–178.

Gardella, J. H., Fisher, B. W., & Teurbe-Tolon, A. R. (2017). A systematic review and meta-analysis of cyber-victimization and educational outcomes for adolescents. *Review of Educational Research, 87*(2), 283–308.

Gewertz, C. (2019, March 20). "Action civics" enlists students in hands-on democracy. *Education Week, 38*(26). Retrieved from edweek.org/ew/articles/2019/03/20/action-civics-enlists-students-in-hands-on-democracy.html

Goldschmidt, P., & Wang, J. (1999). When can schools affect dropout behavior? A longitudinal multilevel analysis. *American Education Research Journal, 36*, 715–738.

Good, T. L. (1987). Two decades of research on teacher expectations: Findings and future directions. *Journal of Teacher Education, 38*(4), 32–47.

Graves, M., Juel, C., Graves, B., & Dewitz, P. (2011). *Teaching reading in the 21st century: Motivation for all learners* (5th ed.). Boston, MA: Pearson.

Guthrie, J. T., Hoa, A.L.W., Wigfield, A., Tonks, S. M., Humenick, N. M., & Littles, E. (2007). Reading motivation and reading comprehension growth in the later elementary years. *Contemporary Educational Psychology, 32*(3), 282–313.

Harste, J., Short, K., & Burke, C. (1988). *Creating classrooms for authors.* Portsmouth, NH: Heinemann.

Harvey, S., & Daniels, H. (2009). *Comprehension and collaboration: Inquiry circles in action.* Portsmouth, NH: Heinemann.

Hattie, J. (2009). *Visible learning: A synthesis of over 800 meta-analyses relating to achievement.* New York, NY: Routledge.

Hattie, J. (2018). *Visible learning plus: 250+ influences on student achievement.* Retrieved from us.corwin.com/sites/default/files/250_influences_10.1 .2018.pdf

Henderson, N. (2013). Havens of resilience. *Educational Leadership, 71*(1), 22–27.

Hendrickx, M.M.H.G., Mainhard, T., Oudman, S., Boor-Klip, H. J., & Brekelmans, M. (2017). Teacher behavior and peer liking and disliking: The teacher as a social referent for peer status. *Journal of Educational Psychology, 109*(4), 546–558.

Henning-Stout, M., James, S., & Macintosh, S. (2000). Reducing harassment of lesbian, gay, bisexual, transgender, and questioning youth in schools. *School Psychology Review, 29*(2), 180–191.

Herr, E. L. (1999). *Counseling in a dynamic society. Contexts and practices for the 21st century.* Alexandria, VA: American Counseling Association.

Herrenkohl, L. R., & Cornelius, L. (2013). Investigating elementary students' scientific and historical argumentation. *Journal of the Learning Sciences, 22*(3), 413–461. doi: 10.1080/10508406.2013.799475

Holmes, M. R., Yoon, S., Berg, K. A., Cage, J. L., & Perzynski, A. T. (2018). Promoting the development of resilient academic functioning in maltreated children. *Child Abuse & Neglect, 75*, 92–103.

Irvin, J. L., Meltzer, J., & Dukes, M. (2007). *Taking action on adolescent literacy: An implementation guide for school leaders.* Alexandria, VA: ASCD.

Israel, E. (2002). Examining multiple perspectives in literature. In J. Holden & J. S. Schmit (Eds.), *Inquiry and the literary text: Constructing discussions in the English classroom* (pp. 89–103). Urbana, IL: National Council of Teachers of English.

Ivey, G. (2002). Getting started: Manageable literacy practices. *Educational Leadership, 60*(3), 20–23.

Ivey, G., & Broaddus, K. (2001). "Just plain reading": A survey of what makes students want to read in middle school classrooms. *Reading Research Quarterly, 36*(4), 350–377.

Ivey, G., & Johnston, P. H. (2013). Engagement with young adult literature: Outcomes and processes. *Reading Research Quarterly, 48*(3), 255–275.

Ivey, G., & Johnston, P. (2018). Engaging disturbing books. *Journal of Adolescent & Adult Literacy, 62*(2), 143–150.

Jerome, E. M., Hamre, B. K., & Pianta, R. C. (2008). Teacher–student relationships from kindergarten to sixth grade: Early childhood predictors of teacher-perceived conflict and closeness. *Social Development, 18*(4), 1467–1507.

Jones, S., Bailey, R., Brush, K., & Kahn, J. (2018). *Preparing for effective SEL implementation.* Cambridge, MA: Harvard Graduate School of Education.

Kackar-Cam, H., & Schmidt, J. (2014). Community-based service-learning as a context for youth autonomy, competence, and relatedness. *High School Journal, 98*(1), 83–108.

Kalafat, J. (2003). School approaches to youth suicide prevention. *American Behavioral Scientist, 46*, 1211–1223.

Kanter, R. M. (1993). *Men and women of the corporation* (2nd ed.). New York, NY: Basic Books.

Kerawalla, L., Littleton, K., Scanlon, E., Jones, A., Gaved, M., Collins, T., . . . Petrou, M. (2013). Personal inquiry learning trajectories in geography: Technological support across contexts. *Interactive Learning Environments, 21*(6), 497–515.

Kim, Y. A. (2003). Necessary social skills related to peer acceptance. *Childhood Education, 79*(4), 234–238.

Kirk, C. M., Lewis, R. K., Brown, K., Karibo, B., & Park, E. (2016). The power of student empowerment: Measuring classroom predictors and individual indicators. *Journal of Educational Research, 109*(6), 589–595.

Kleinfeld, J. (1975). Effective teachers of Eskimo and Indian students. *School Review, 83*, 301–344.

Kolb, D. (1984). *Experiential learning: Experience as the source of learning and development.* Englewood Cliffs, NJ: Prentice Hall.

Kotok, S., Ikoma, S., & Bodovski, K. (2016). School climate and dropping out of school in the era of accountability. *American Journal of Education, 122*(4), 569–599.

Kovac, S. H., & Range, L. M. (2000). Writing projects: Lessening undergraduates' unique suicidal bereavement. *Suicide and Life-Threatening Behavior, 30*(1), 50–60.

Ladson-Billings, G. (1995). Toward a theory of culturally relevant pedagogy. *American Educational Research Journal, 32*, 465–491.

Larson, L. (2009). Reader response meets new literacies: Empowering readers in online learning communities. *The Reading Teacher, 62*(8), 638–648.

Leitch, L. (2017). Action steps using ACEs and trauma-informed care: A resilience model. *Health and Justice, 5*(5), 1–10.

Lent, R. C. (2016). *This is disciplinary literacy: Reading, writing, thinking, and doing . . . content area by content area.* Thousand Oaks, CA: Corwin.

Lent, R. C., & Voigt, M. M. (2019). *Disciplinary literacy in action: How to create and sustain a school-wide culture of deep reading, writing, and thinking.* Thousand Oaks, CA: Corwin.

Lesh, B. A. (2011). *Why won't you just tell us the answer? Teaching historical thinking in grades 7–12.* Portland, ME: Stenhouse.

Levy, B. L. M., Thomas, E. E., Drago, K., & Rex, L. A. (2013). Examining studies of inquiry-based learning in three fields of education: Sparking generative conversation. *Journal of Teacher Education, 64*(5), 387–408.

Littlefield, R. S. (2001). High school student perceptions of the efficacy of debate participation. *Argumentation and Advocacy, 38*(2), 83–97. doi: 10.1080/00028533.2001.11821559

Los Angeles County Office of Education. (2008). *TESA coordinator manual.* Los Angeles, CA: Author.

Louie, B. (2005). Development of empathetic responses with multicultural literature. *Journal of Adolescent & Adult Literacy, 48*(7), 566–578.

Mahoney, J. L., Durlak, J. A., & Weissberg, R. P. (2018). An update on social and emotional learning outcome research. *Phi Delta Kappan, 100*(4), 18–23.

Malin, H. (2011). American identity development and citizenship education: A summary of perspectives and call for new research. *Applied Developmental Science, 15*(2), 111–116.

Marshall, J. C. (2013). *Succeeding with inquiry in science and math classrooms.* Alexandria, VA: Association for Supervision and Curriculum Development.

Marshall, J. C. (2016). *The highly effective teacher: 7 classroom-tested practices that foster student success.* Alexandria, VA: Association for Supervision and Curriculum Development.

Martin, W.B.W. (1987). Students' perceptions of causes and consequences of embarrassment in the school. *Canadian Journal of Education, 12,* 277–293.

Masten, A. S., Best, K. M., & Garmezy, N. (1990). Resilience and development: Contributions from the study of children who overcome adversity. *Development and Psychopathology, 2,* 425–444.

McLeod, J. D., Uemura, R., & Rohrman, S. (2012). Adolescent mental health, behavior problems, and academic achievement. *Journal of Health and Social Behavior, 53*(4), 482–497.

Montague, M., & Rinaldi, C. (2001). Classroom dynamics and children at risk: A followup. *Learning Disability Quarterly, 24*(2), 75–83.

Moon, J. (2004). *A handbook of reflective and experiential learning: Theory and practice.* London, England: Routledge Falmer.

Moonie, S., Sterling, D. A., Figgs, L. W., & Castro, M. (2008). The relationship between school absence, academic performance, and asthma status. *Journal of School Health, 78*(3), 140–148.

Morgenstern, C. (1918). *Stufen: Eine entwickelung in aphorismen und tagebuch-notizen* [Project Gutenberg e-book]. Retrieved from gutenberg.org/etext/15898

National Action Civics Collaborative. (2010). Action civics: A declaration for rejuvenating our democratic traditions. Retrieved from actioncivicscollaborative.org/about-us/action-civics-declaration/

National Child Traumatic Stress Network. (n.d.). *Secondary traumatic stress.* Retrieved from nctsn.org/trauma-informed-care/secondary-traumatic-stress.

National Institute of Mental Health. (2019). *Mental health information: Statistics suicide.* Retrieved from nimh.nih.gov/health/statistics/suicide.shtml.

National Youth Leadership Council. (n.d.). *What is service-learning?* Retrieved from nylc.org/page/WhatisService-Learning?&hhsearchterms=%22is+and+service+and+learning%22

Niedzwiedz, C., Haw, C., Hawton, K., & Platt, S. (2014). The definition and epidemiology of clusters of suicidal behavior: A systematic review. *Suicide & Life-Threatening Behavior, 44*(5), 569–581.

Nieto, S. (2018). *Language, culture, and teaching: Critical perspectives* (3rd ed.). New York, NY: Routledge.

O'Dougherty Wright, M., Masten, A. S., & Narayan, A. J. (2013). Resilience processes in development: Four waves of research on positive adaptation in the context of adversity. In S. Goldstein & R. B. Brooks (Eds.), *Handbook of resilience in children* (pp. 15–38). New York, NY: Springer.

Oyserman, D., Terry, K., & Bybee, D. (2002). A possible selves intervention to enhance school involvement. *Journal of Adolescence, 25*(3), 313–326. Retrieved from doi.org/10.1006/jado.2002.0474

Partnership for 21st Century Skills. (2013). *Framework for 21st century learners.* Retrieved from battelleforkids.org/networks/p21

Perry, B. D. (2014). *Helping traumatized children: A brief overview for caregivers.* Houston, TX: Child Trauma Academy.

Pianta, R. C. (1992). *The student-teacher relationship scale.* Charlottesville, VA: University of Virginia.

Pitcher, S. M., Albright, L. K., DeLaney, C. J., Walker, N. T., Seumarinesingh, K., Mogge, S., . . . Dunston, P. J. (2007). Assessing adolescents' motivation to read. *Journal of Adolescent & Adult Literacy, 50*(5), 378–396.

Plumb, J. L., Bush, K. A., & Kersevich, S. E. (2016). Trauma-sensitive schools: An evidence-based approach. *School Social Work Journal, 40*(2), 37–60.

Potter, S., & Davis, B. H. (2003). A first-year teacher implements class meetings. *Kappa Delta Pi Record, 39*(2), 88–90.

Priniski, S. J., Hecht, C. A., & Harackiewicz, J. M. (2018). Making learning personally meaningful: A new framework for relevance research. *Journal of Experimental Education, 86*(1), 11–29.

Ritchart, R., Church, M., & Morrison, K. (2011). *Making thinking visible: How to promote engagement and independence for all learners.* San Francisco, CA: Jossey-Bass.

Rodriguez, R. J. (2019). *Teaching culturally sustaining and inclusive young adult literature: Critical perspectives and conversations.* New York, NY: Routledge.

Rosenblatt, L. M. (1978). *The reader, the text, the poem: The transactional theory of the literary work.* Carbondale: Southern Illinois University Press.

Rumberger, R. W. (1995). Dropping out of middle school: A multilevel analysis of students and schools. *American Educational Research Journal, 32*, 583–625.

Ruzek, E. A., Hafen, C. A., Allen, J. P., Gregory, A., Mikami, A. Y., & Pianta, R. C. (2016). How teacher emotional support motivates students: The mediating roles of perceived peer relatedness, autonomy support, and competence. *Learning & Instruction, 42*, 95–103.

Salloum, S., Goddard, R., & Larsen, R. (2017). Social capital in schools: A conceptual and empirical analysis of the equity of its distribution and relation to academic development. *Teachers College Record, 119*, 1–29.

Sandelowski. M., & Barroso, J. (2002). Finding the findings in qualitative studies. *Journal of Nursing Scholarship, 34*(3), 213–219.

Sanders, J., Munford, R., & Liebenberg, L. (2016). The role of teachers in building resilience of at risk youth. *International Journal of Educational Research, 80*, 111–123.

Savitz, R. S., & Wallace, K. (2016). Using the inquiry process to motivate and engage all (including struggling) readers. *The Clearing House: A Journal of Educational Strategies, Issues and Ideas, 89*(3), 91–96. doi: 10.1080/00098655.2016.1184923

Schoeler, T., Duncan L., Ploubidis, G. B., Cecil, C. M., & Pingault, J-B. (2018). Quasi-experimental evidence on short- and long-term consequences of bullying victimization: A meta-analysis. *Psychological Bulletin, 144*(12), 1229–1246.

Schultz, B. D. (2017). *Teaching in the cracks: Openings and opportunities for student-centered, action-focused curriculum.* New York, NY: Teachers College Press.

Shapira-Lishchinsky, O., & Tsemach, S. (2014). Psychological empowerment as a mediator between teachers' perceptions of authentic leadership and their withdrawal and citizenship behaviors. *Educational Administration Quarterly, 50*(4), 675–712.

Shor, I. (1999). What is critical literacy? *Journal of Pedagogy, Pluralism, and Practice, 1*(4), 2–32.

Singham, T., Viding, E., Schoeler, T., Arseneault, L., Ronald, A., Cecil, C. M., . . . Pingault, J-B. (2017). Concurrent and longitudinal contribution of exposure to bullying in childhood to mental health: The role of vulnerability and resilience. *Journal of the American Medical Association Psychiatry, 74*, 1112–1119.

Sisk, V. F., Burgoyne, A. P., Sun, J., Bulter, J. L., & Macnamara, B. N. (2018). To what extent and under which circumstances are growth mind-sets important to academic achievement? Two meta-analyses. *Psychological Science, 29*(4), 549–571.

Smith, D., Fisher, D., & Frey, N. (2015). *Better than carrots or sticks: Restorative practices for positive classroom management.* Alexandria, VA: Association for Supervision and Curriculum Development.

Smith, M., & Wilhelm, J. D. (2004). "I just like being good at it": The importance of competence in the literate lives of young men. *Journal of Adolescent & Adult Literacy, 47*(6), 454–461.

Split, J. L., Hughes, J. N., Wu, J. Y., & Kwok, O. M. (2012). Dynamics of teacher–student relationships: Stability and change across elementary school and the influence on children's academic success. *Child Development, 83*(4), 1180–1195.

Substance Abuse and Mental Health Services Administration. (2014). *SAM-HSA's concept of trauma and guidance for a trauma-informed approach.* HHS Publication No. (SMA) 14-4884. Rockville, MD: Author.

Tai, T., & Bame, S. (2011). Cost–benefit analysis of childhood asthma management through school-based clinic programs. *Journal of Community Health, 36*(2), 253–260.

Tatum, A. W. (2015). Writing through the labyrinth of fears: A legacy of Walter Dean Myers. *Journal of Adolescent & Adult Literacy, 58*(7), 536–540.

Thomas, K., & Velthouse, B. (1990). Cognitive elements of empowerment: An "interpretive" model of intrinsic task motivation. *Academy of Management Review, 15*, 666–681.

Trauma and Learning Policy Initiative. (n.d.). Helping traumatized children learn: Frequently asked questions about trauma-sensitive schools. Retrieved from traumasensitiveschools.org/frequently-asked-questions/

Turner, J. C., Midgley, C., Meyer, D. K., Gheen, M., Anderman, E. M., Kang, Y., & Patrick, H. (2002). The classroom environment and students' reports of avoidance strategies in mathematics: A multimethod study. *Journal of Educational Psychology, 94*, 88–106.

Valentino, M. J. (1996). Responding when a life depends on it: What to write in the margins when students self-disclose. *Teaching English in the Two-Year College, 23*, 274–283.

van der Kolk, B. (2014). *The body keeps the score: Brain, mind, and body in the healing of trauma.* New York, NY: Viking.

Ware, F. (2006). Warm demander pedagogy: Culturally responsive teaching that supports a culture of achievement for African American students. *Urban Education, 41*(4), 427–456.

Warner, E., & Bruschke, J. (2001). Gone on debating: Competitive academic debate as a tool of empowerment for urban America. *Contemporary Argumentation and Debate, 22*, 1–21.

Waters, E., & Sroufe, L. A. (1983). Social competence as a developmental construct. *Developmental Review, 3,* 79–97.

Watts, R. J., & Flanagan, C. (2007). Pushing the envelope on youth civic engagement: A developmental and liberation psychology perspective. *Journal of Community Psychology, 35*(6), 779–792.

Weber, K., Martin, M. M., & Cayanus, J. L. (2005). Student interest: A two-study re-examination of the concept. *Communication Quarterly, 53*(1), 71–86.

Wilder, P. (2019). Conversations with myself: Literacy as a conscious tool of healing. *English Journal, 108*(3), 60–66.

Wilhelm, J. D. (2001). *Improving comprehension with think-aloud strategies.* New York, NY: Scholastic.

Wilhelm, J. D., Douglas, W., & Fry, S. W. (2014). *The activist learner: Inquiry, literacy, and service to make learning better.* New York, NY: Teachers College Press.

Wilhelm, J. D., & Novak, B. (2011). *Teaching literacy for love and wisdom: Being the book and being the change.* New York, NY: Teachers College Press.

Wilhelm, J. D., & Smith, M. W. (1996). *"You gotta BE the book": Teaching engaged and reflective reading with adolescents.* New York, NY: Teachers College Press.

Wilson, B. L., & Corbett, H. D. (2001). *Listening to urban kids: School reform and the teachers they want.* Albany, NY: State University of New York Press.

Wineburg, S. (1999). Historical thinking and other unnatural acts. *Phi Delta Kappan, 80*(7), 488–499.

Wlodkowski, R. J. (1983). *Motivational opportunities for successful teaching* [Leader's guide]. Phoenix, AZ: Universal Dimensions.

Wolfsdorf, A. (2018). When it comes to high school English, let's put away the triggers. *English Journal, 108*(1), 39–44.

W. K. Kellogg Foundation. (2004). *Logic model development guide.* Battle Creek, MI: Author.

Wright, J., & Man, C. C. (2001). Mastery or mystery? Therapeutic writing: A review of the literature. *British Journal of Guidance & Counselling, 29,* 277–291.

Index

About the Authors

Douglas Fisher, Ph.D., is a professor and chair of the department of Educational Leadership at San Diego State University and a teacher leader at Health Sciences High and Middle College after having been an early intervention teacher and elementary school educator. He is the recipient of an International Reading Association William S. Grey citation of merit, an Exemplary Leader award from the Conference on English Leadership of NCTE, as well as a Christa McAuliffe award for excellence in teacher education. He has published numerous articles on reading and literacy, differentiated instruction, and curriculum design as well as books, such as *PLC+: Better Decisions and Greater Impact by Design, Building Equity*, and *Assessment-Capable Learners*. He can be reached at dfisher@mail.sdsu.edu.

Nancy Frey, Ph.D., is a professor in educational leadership at San Diego State University and the recipient of the 2008 Early Career Achievement Award from the Literacy Research Association. Nancy has published in numerous articles on subjects related to literacy, equity, and schooling as well as books such as *Teacher Clarity Playbook, All Learning Is Social and Emotional*, and *Engagement by Design: Creating Learning Environments Where Students Thrive*. She is a member of the Literacy Research Panel of the International Literacy Association. Nancy is a credentialed special educator, reading specialist, and administrator in California, and is a co-founder and administrator at Health Sciences High and Middle College. She can be reached at nfrey@sdsu.edu.

Rachelle S. Savitz, Ph.D., is an assistant professor of adolescent literacy at Clemson University after having been a K-12 literacy coach and interventionist and high school reading teacher. She is the recipient of American Reading Forum's Gary Moorman Early Career Literacy Scholar Award, finalist for the International Literacy Association's Timothy and Cynthia Shanahan Outstanding Dissertation award, as well as Secondary Reading Council of Florida's Reading Teacher of the Year award. She has published articles on inquiry-based learning, analysis and use of young adult literature, and response to intervention. She can be reached at rsavitz@clemson.edu.